# Enjoy Satisfying Relationships

TIME
LIFE
BOOKS

MINDPOWER
JOURNEY THROUGH THE MIND AND BODY
COOKERY AROUND THE WORLD
LOST CIVILIZATIONS
THE ILLUSTRATED LIBRARY OF THE EARTH
SYSTEM EARTH
LIBRARY OF CURIOUS AND UNUSUAL FACTS
BUILDING BLOCKS
A CHILD'S FIRST LIBRARY OF LEARNING
VOYAGE THROUGH THE UNIVERSE
THE THIRD REICH
MYSTERIES OF THE UNKNOWN
TIME-LIFE HISTORY OF THE WORLD
FITNESS, HEALTH & NUTRITION
HEALTHY HOME COOKING
UNDERSTANDING COMPUTERS
THE ENCHANTED WORLD
LIBRARY OF NATIONS
PLANET EARTH
THE GOOD COOK
THE WORLD'S WILD PLACES

# MINDPOWER

## Enjoy Satisfying Relationships

TIME-LIFE BOOKS
Amsterdam

MINDPOWER

Created, edited, and designed by DK Direct Limited,
23-24 Henrietta Street, London WC2E 8NA

A DORLING KINDERSLEY BOOK

**DK DIRECT LIMITED**

**Managing Editor** Jane Laing
**Senior Editor** Sue Leonard
**Editor** Claire Calman

**Managing Art Editor** Ruth Shane
**Art Editor** Sarah Crosbie
**Designers** Piers Tilbury, Sue Caws

**Editorial Director** Jonathan Reed
**Design Director** Ed Day
**Production Manager** Ian Paton

**Editorial Consultants** Reg Grant, Sarah Litvinoff
**Contributors** Vida Adamoli, Claire Calman, Julia Cole,
Sarah Litvinoff, Laura Marcus, Ruth Shane, Kate Swainson

**TIME-LIFE BOOKS EUROPEAN EDITION**
**Staff for Enjoy Satisfying Relationships**

**Design Director** Mary Staples
**Editorial Production** Emma Wishart
European edition edited by Ellen Phillips

First Time-Life European English language edition 1995
ISBN 0 7054 1626 7
TIME-LIFE is a trademark of Time-Warner Inc., U.S.A.

Printed by GEA, Milan, and bound by GEP, Cremona, Italy

30  29  28  27  26  25  24  23  22  21  20  19  18  17  16  15  14  13  12  11  10  9  8  7  6  5  4  3  2

# CONTENTS

# INTRODUCTION

FOR MOST OF US, few things are more rewarding than the pleasure we derive from our relationships—with partners, with friends, with family, with colleagues—and even from the more fleeting contact we have with people whose lives touch our own in passing. As with anything that affects us deeply, however, relationships can also be a source of anxiety, frustration, and unhappiness. So, how do you reap the enormous potential for happiness that relationships can offer? And how do you minimize the pain they cause?

*Enjoy Satisfying Relationships* helps you explore your relationship patterns. Chapter One focuses on each of the vital levels of friendship—from the casual acquaintance with whom you exchange pleasantries to the close friend who shares your most intimate thoughts. Evaluating the structure of your friendship network can help you appreciate the importance of those around you, or it may lead you to conclude that you would benefit from changing certain aspects of your relationships.

Closest to the center of your relationship network, your most intimate and loving partnerships bring a wonderful sense of stability and contentment to your life, but they may also be the cause of major unhappiness and frustration. Chapter Two looks at why this is the case. What is love? Is there one definition that applies to everyone or does each individual experience love differently? Although there are no set rules governing which relationships will work, it is possible to see why some people are compatible and why other combinations are disastrous. This chapter helps you to examine your past relationships—their strengths and weaknesses—so that you can understand what you really want from a partner and how you can influence future choices.

If you are involved in a relationship, how well do you know one another? Do you communicate well? Do you manage to deal with difficult issues by negotiating in a mature manner, or do you react in ways that lead to anger and recrimination? It is possible to alter the way you respond to conflict with your partner so that you do not take differences of opinion as a personal insult. Chapter Three enables you to make your relationship more fulfilling, first by giving you the means to understand each other better, and then by providing you with skills to improve the communication between you. With consideration and understanding, a healthy relationship should be able to survive disagreements and thrive on change and growth, emerging enhanced and strengthened.

In our supposedly enlightened world, it is surprising how many old sexual myths still survive. Chapter Four encourages you to discover how comprehensive your sexual knowledge really is and to assess how satisfied you are with your sex life. It shows you how to express your sexual needs and desires clearly and in a non-confrontational way, enabling you and your partner to get the best out of your sex life, whether you are involved in a long-standing union or embarking on a new liaison.

*Enjoy Satisfying Relationships* helps you identify any areas of frustration and dissatisfaction in your relationship network so that you can improve them, and enables you to learn from the satisfying and emotionally balanced relationships that you do have. It guides you toward creating and maintaining healthy and fulfilling partnerships with all sorts of people in your life, from colleagues and friends to your intimate partner. Begin by assessing the quality of your network now by completing your relationship map (see over).

# MAKING A RELATIONSHIP MAP

H OW CLOSE ARE YOU to the people you know? How do you perceive your relationships? Are they as you would like them to be, or do you wish you could be closer to some people, more distant from others? Relationships are intangible in many ways, and it is often difficult to identify areas that cause frustration or unhappiness. Making a "relationship map" helps you determine which of your relationships would benefit from your active intervention, either to strengthen or consolidate them or, in some cases, to make them less intense or dominating. To familiarize yourself with the structure and function of a relationship map, look closely at the examples provided, then read the accompanying comments, which come from both the people who drew the maps, and a professional relationship counselor.

## Drawing your own map

Draw a relationship map for yourself: Make a series of concentric circles and place yourself in the center. Now consider all the people with whom you feel you have some sort of relationship—partner, family, friends, colleagues, and people connected to you in some other way. Place those who are closest to you emotionally nearest to you geographically on your map: for example, your partner or children might appear in the center with you or in the adjacent ring, while more distant relatives or your boss might fall well away from you in an outer ring. There is no right or wrong pattern: the aim is to highlight how you perceive your relationship with each of these people. Forget about how you think these relationships should be or, for the moment, what you would ideally like them to be; do not think about how people feel toward you, just record your relationships as you see them in terms of closeness.

Once you have completed your map, consider which people you found hard to place and whether you were surprised by the positions in which you put people. Analyzing your placements will reveal how you feel at the moment about your relationships: you may well find that your map will be different if you do it again in a year's time, or even in just a couple of months.

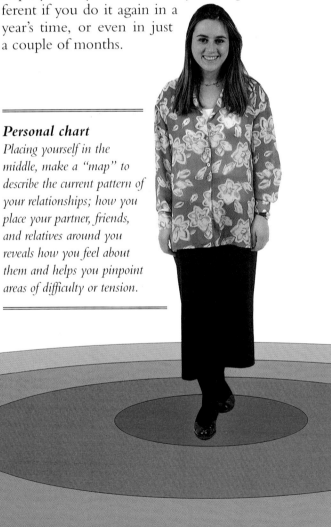

### Personal chart

*Placing yourself in the middle, make a "map" to describe the current pattern of your relationships; how you place your partner, friends, and relatives around you reveals how you feel about them and helps you pinpoint areas of difficulty or tension.*

Ask yourself the following questions:
• Is your partner closer/farther away than you would like?
• Are your children closer/farther away than you would like?
• Are your parents closer/farther away than you would like?
• Are your relatives closer/farther away than you would like?
• Are your colleagues closer/farther away than you would like?
• Are there people on your map whom you would rather exclude?
• Would you like to see more friends on your map?
• Are there people you have left off whom you would have included a year ago?

It may seem calculating, but asking yourself these sorts of questions will help you assess how content you are with the current state of your relationships. You can then work on increasing the intimacy of some relationships, and distancing those people who no longer play a significant part in your life. You may find it helpful to do another map that shows how you would like your relationships to be—your ideal map. Look at the two maps side by side and identify the areas you want to improve.

## Using your map
Think about the people who are more distant on your map than they would have been in the past, and those who are absent. Why do you feel that you are less close to them now? Have you made a conscious decision to distance these people, or have those relationships slipped away from you?

Consider the relationships that you would like to be closer—perhaps those with friends or colleagues, or those with particular members of your family. Make a plan of action, noting down ideas on how you could strengthen the links between you. For example, you might decide to ask a colleague out to lunch or to a concert or a movie after work. You could try to deepen a friendship by sharing something more personal about your life or feelings, and encouraging the other person to do the same.

Are you comfortable with the distance between yourself and your partner? Do you feel that this distance has widened or narrowed over the last two years/five years? It could be beneficial to use your relationship map as a trigger to explore more deeply areas and feelings that may be troubling you.

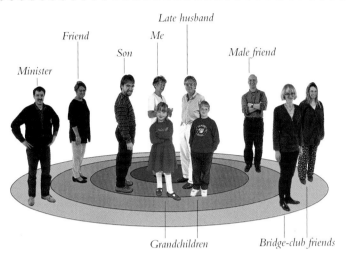

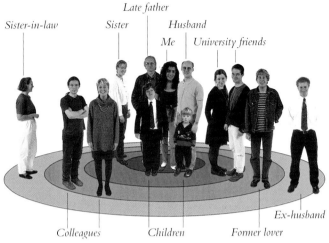

**1. Harriet:** "I haven't been able to imagine ever being as close to anyone again since my husband died, although I felt my son was totally part of me when he was young. I don't see my son and grandchildren as much as I'd like really. Perhaps friends should play a greater part in my life than they do now—I think I could put more energy into friendships, and I might get more from them."

**3. Jonie:** "When completing my relationship map, I was aware that I've made some progress: I feel I've managed to distance people who I've wanted to move farther away, like my ex-husband, who cannot detach himself from me. I felt happy putting my children and husband clustered around me. My father is no longer alive, but I feel he's still very much with me so he has a place on my map."

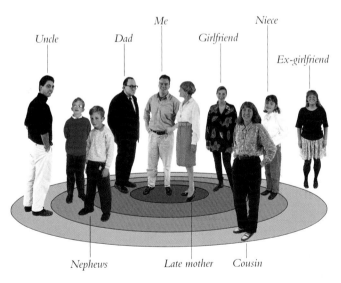

**2. John:** "I feel relatives should be close, so I felt a bit guilty about putting uncles etc. so far out. I do see the family as very central and I'm pleased about that. I'm surprised that I consider my ex as being important, but she does mean something to me, and I thought I would have put other friends closer in. It shows you who really matters to you."

**4. Neil:** "My ex-partner and current partner are close to one another, rather worryingly, but it does not surprise me. I feel close to my ex as we were together for several years. I cannot see my current partner getting any closer, which is a bit disappointing, though I feel it's better to face up to that now rather than expect too much in the future."

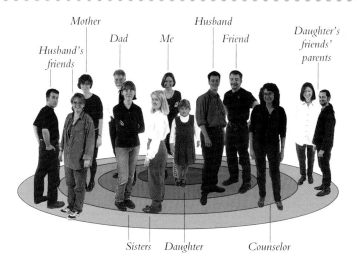

*Mother* *Husband* *Daughter's friends' parents* *Husband's friends* *Dad* *Me* *Friend*

*Sisters* *Daughter* *Counselor*

**5. Pat:** "When I first met my husband, I would definitely have put him in the center with me. Now I feel the bond with my daughter is the most important relationship in my life. My husband and I are close, but I often turn to my best friend or to my Dad when I need to talk. I'm also seeing a counselor at the moment, and I trust her totally and feel I can just let go and talk about anything with her. I feel rather sad that my mother and sister aren't closer, but we've never really been a close family."

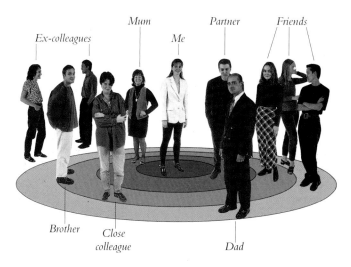

*Ex-colleagues* *Mum* *Partner* *Friends* *Me*

*Brother* *Close colleague* *Dad*

**6. Susan:** "I felt I wanted to put my partner in the center but resisted being too much a part of someone else, being too interdependent. I've learned lessons from the past about that. I notice how little I miss my ex-colleagues and this surprises me; I think I associate them with a previous stage in my life and I feel I've moved on now."

## Our counselor's comments:

**1. Harriet:** This map shows how coping with bereavement is an ongoing task, which takes some time to accomplish. Only Harriet's dead husband is intimately close. Her male friend stands alone, which could indicate ambivalence toward him. Building on her friendships could improve Harriet's confidence. It could also prepare her for a closer relationship with the lone man, if desired, in the future.

**2. John:** The position of John's late mother indicates the special place she occupies in his heart, but his girlfriend seems to be moving into this important area. He could interpret this as a threat, or it might imply that their relationship is becoming more important. John seems to be on the verge of making a commitment outside the family, which he may find difficult but ultimately rewarding.

**3. Jonie:** The huddle of people in the center of this map could illustrate Jonie's need of protection, and a desire to be defended from outside influences, notably her ex. She might need to work on her assertiveness, in order to face potentially difficult issues connected to those people on her outer ring.

**4. Neil:** There is a sense of resignation in Neil's comments. The distance between people could mean that he feels unsupported, and even lonely. His isolation may be a defence against hurt. The break-up with his ex-partner seems to have been more painful than he admitted. In order to assess expectations of future relationships, he needs to analyze more closely his feelings toward his ex, and his current partner.

**5. Pat:** The key position of Pat's daughter in the center ring is important. In an attempt to achieve the warmth she lacked as a child, Pat has assigned her daughter a difficult role. The daughter is likely to feel stifled by such an intimate relationship, and the mother devastated when she eventually leaves home. Moves toward recreating the past closeness between husband and wife could offer a more balanced view of the present relationships.

**6. Susan:** The people here are evenly distributed, suggesting a balanced view of friends and family. It may also indicate that Susan hides her emotions. The lack of intimate relationships shows self-reliance, but at a cost. Her tough exterior may make it hard for others to be warm toward her. She might benefit from understanding her vulnerability, and realizing how risk-taking in relationships can be worthwhile.

# CHAPTER ONE

# YOUR FRIENDSHIP NETWORK

YOU ARE AS DEPENDENT upon your relationships with other human beings as you are on food, clothing, and shelter. Perhaps the worst deprivation that people can be made to suffer is not that of food, liberty, or even of life but of company: enforced solitary confinement has been known to drive people mad.

The company of other people is one of the mainstays of our existence, providing not just simple companionship, but also the rewards of sharing both good times and bad: conversation and laughter, understanding, sympathy, and support. It also gives us something less tangible but no less important: a sense of connection with other people, of being a valued part of a larger framework.

Chapter One explores the many types of relationship that exist, all of which are important for our development, sense of well-being, and general happiness. Your most intimate friends, your casual acquaintances, your close family members, your distant relatives, colleagues you work with daily, people you are on nodding terms with—all form a part of your relationship network, and this chapter will help you examine each one. It also shows you how to identify the particular kind of relationship you favor (see the "Friendship Preferences" quiz, pp. 36-37) and guides you to a better understanding of your relationship needs.

Even the greatest friendships are not without troubles so, as well as exploring the benefits each type of friendship can confer, this chapter examines the kind of difficulties that may crop up, and discusses ways of handling them. "Coping with Negative Feelings" (see pp. 32-35) shows the importance of keeping friendships in good repair and of tackling problems such as envy or resentment before they inflict permanent damage; while "The Golden Rules of Friendship" (p. 27) gives guidelines on how to be a good friend.

This chapter also looks at what intimacy means in friendship. Although the word intimacy is often used to convey physical contact, it does not just mean sex. It means an all-accepting closeness, trust, and understanding between two people. You can find this kind of intimacy with friends and family members as well as with a partner. Almost all of us crave intimacy, and it can be a source of tremendous happiness and fulfillment. Discover how to make the most of the people in your life: how to form casual friendships, and how to develop and deepen your bonds with others.

FRIENDSHIPS ARE A VITAL SOURCE OF EMOTIONAL SUSTENANCE. AS WELL AS PROVIDING THE PLEASURE OF COMPANIONSHIP, YOUR FRIENDSHIP NETWORK OFFERS YOU A SENSE OF SUPPORT AND BELONGING.

# FRIENDSHIP CATEGORIES

ONE OF THE MOST EFFECTIVE ways of punishing or even torturing a human being is by depriving him or her of human contact. In fact, people who are isolated for extended periods—for example, prisoners in solitary confinement—have been known to dream and hallucinate that other people are there with them, so vital is the need for interaction with others.

So contact is a basic human need. It lies behind the importance of friendships of all kinds. The strangers you encounter in everyday life—at the store, in the subway, waiting at table—as well as your closest friends, all provide you with essential contact and support. Friends can help to give you a sense of belonging, practical and psychological support, emotional stability, and, of course, the opportunity to share activities and enjoy conversation and laughter. Yet friendships vary considerably in nature, and operate on many different levels. You wouldn't expect the person you regularly chat with about the weather as you wait in line for the bus to offer you emotional support. But even the lightweight conversation that such acquaintances provide brings an essential element to the framework of your life.

## Types of friendship

Friendships can be categorized into the following groups according to intimacy: acquaintances, friends by association, colleagues, and close friends.

Acquaintances consist of people you know only vaguely and with whom you discuss only impersonal subjects. You tend to keep these individuals at a distance; you probably do not discuss personal issues with them. The superficial, easy-going nature of these relationships is comforting and offers reassurance that life continues in a normal way even when you are experiencing the most traumatic personal events.

Friends by association are those people you are close to because of a shared interest or lifestyle. Roommates at college, with whom you share so much during two or three years of your life, fall into this category: although you have much in common at the time, you find that very little remains once you make your separate ways in the adult world. In the same way, a group of mothers with small children may become very close friends as their offspring make the traumatic and demanding progression through infancy and toddlerhood. But once their children start school and develop their own friends, the mothers often discover that the only common interest they shared was their children. Similarly, friends that you make on vacation—even if you get on very well with them for two weeks—may have little to offer should you meet on your home ground.

It is possible to forge extremely rewarding friendships in the workplace. Work is often much more than a source of income. It provides companionship and instantly shared activities, as well as relationships that can easily develop beyond the work environment. However, in many cases, friendships with work colleagues may not last beyond the comradeship of a shared endeavor: they may be no more than friends by association.

### A friendship structure

*Your friendships are constantly shifting. As new acquaintances arrive on the scene so you develop deeper relationships with people you had known only on a superficial level, and lose contact with friends whose interests you no longer share.*

## SURVEY YOUR FRIENDSHIPS

It is a useful exercise to complete a survey of the types of friendships you have, where they originated, how they have changed over time, and what needs they meet for you.

Write a list of your friend's names, placing them in the following categories: close friends; friends by association with whom you share a common interest; colleagues; acquaintances. Are there any spaces in your survey? Do you seem to favor a particular type of friendship?  If you are unhappy with what you find, perhaps it is time to make some new friends and find new interests (see "Meeting People" p. 17).

• If you have many acquaintances but very few close friends, you may have trouble getting close to people. You need to work at making new friends, or at getting to know some of your acquaintances better, in order to benefit from the interdependence that close friends share.

• Are all your friends work colleagues? This clearly indicates that your work occupies a major part of your life. Although there is nothing wrong with having friends at work, if all your friends are colleagues, a change in your work situation would leave you isolated. You should try to establish another side to your life, away from work.

• Do you have a great many close friendships? Although they have the potential to provide valuable emotional support, it might be worthwhile considering the way they operate. Do you always seem to be the one doing the listening and the supporting? One vital quality of close friendships is that they involve give and take on both sides, so make sure you're focusing on relationships that offer you support, too.

Close friendships are the most valued of all, and they should survive most of life's traumas and changes. Their nature has no predictable pattern. You may see your close friends every week or you may only be able to get together infrequently, but the strength of your relationship means that you are always able to support and trust each other, understand each other's feelings, show affection, share secrets and offer help.

Often your sexual partner will be your closest friend. No matter how close you are to your partner, however, it is healthy to have other friends, so that you have time away from each other. Otherwise you may feel suffocated; so may your partner.

## Keeping a balance

Friends are not restricted to a particular category. Acquaintances become closer friends. Friends by association disappear from the scene, and a relationship with a work colleague may develop into a deeper, more meaningful friendship.

One American study, which investigated the number of friends that people have, suggested that the average number of friends for an individual is 15. However, when questioned on the number of close friends the subjects had, the number dropped to six. Ultimately, however, it is not the number of friends you have that is important: it is the significance of the roles they play in your life, and the

# MEETING PEOPLE

Sometimes you can make new friends without even trying—via existing friends, perhaps, or through work. Often, however, you have to take a more active approach if you want to expand your social network.

Be aware of potential opportunities for meeting people: always accept invitations to social events; give parties yourself and ask each guest to bring a new person as well; organize outings with colleagues; start a local or work newsletter—this gives you a good excuse to contact people.

Friendships are often struck up over a mutual interest or project. Take advantage of this by becoming involved in activities that particularly interest you. This has two benefits: 1) you will meet people with whom you already have something in common;

2) you are likely to be both enthusiastic and relaxed, so people will see you at your best. Having a shared purpose also makes it easier to start a conversation: ask someone to clarify a point from the lesson or borrow a textbook or a particular piece of equipment. Then open up the conversation by asking questions.

Make an effort to take part in activities that encourage social contact. If you enjoy sport, for example, you would be better joining a tennis or golf club or taking a fencing class than going swimming or jogging. Find out about adult education classes and other activities, such as special interest societies and clubs—local walks, gardening, chess, or photography—from the city hall or public library.

amount of combined support they offer that is so essential. Many people treat their friendships fairly lightly and do not give them the same amount of care and consideration they give to sexual relationships. But friendships make a vital contribution to a balanced, happy existence and warrant a considerable degree of work, thoughtfulness, and respect. As Samuel Johnson (1709-1784) said "A man, Sir, should keep his friendships in good repair."

### Human links

*The companionship of others is essential for a balanced existence. You need your friendships and should value and nurture them.*

# ACQUAINTANCES

All of us have acquaintances —people we know personally and with whom we are happy to stop and chat, but wouldn't necessarily make a special arrangement to meet socially. Your circle of acquaintances includes a very wide range of people: friends of friends, neighbors, your parents' friends, work contacts, perhaps people who have a practical or commercial link with you such as local shopkeepers, your clients or customers, or the parents of your children's friends.

If your social set consists almost entirely of acquaintances, however, it may be that you fear a deeper level of contact and that you are wary of letting people know you. This can make you feel isolated emotionally, so it is worth examining your friendship needs and working on learning how to become closer to other people (see also "Survey Your Friendships," p. 15).

## Respecting boundaries

By definition less close than friends, acquaintances are still an important part of your relationship network. The main distinction between an acquaintance and a friend is a question of boundaries: If you are feeling down, for example, and a friend asked you how you were, you would probably be quite honest; to an acquaintance, however, you would be more likely to reply, "Fine, thanks. How are you?" You might not feel ready to reveal a vulnerable element of your nature, preferring instead to limit your contact to a few amicable exchanges.

Most acquaintances clearly understand the boundaries of intimacy; acquaintanceship tends to be fairly superficial. You might well chat about impersonal topics—holidays, work, leisure interests, the weather—but avoid more personal or contentious ones: your love life, religion, family or money problems, sex, and so on.

It is vital to recognize these boundaries: How would you feel if someone you know only very casually poured his heart out about personal secrets or problems? It would probably make you feel awkward and ill at ease, and, because you don't know the person well, you would be unsure of how to respond to the situation.

*Essential boundaries*

*The undemanding nature of an acquaintanceship depends on the mutual recognition of boundaries—both of you need to be aware of limits to the level of intimacy so that you don't overstep the mark.*

## The advantages of acquaintances

Although contact with an acquaintance is usually less rewarding or interesting than a meeting with a friend, it does have its benefits. Meeting people we know helps us to feel connected with the world and the rest of humanity; this kind of contact is reassuring. It makes us feel less isolated, and it gives us a chance to communicate—to share something with others, even if it's only a brief conversation.

Another benefit depends on the very limits imposed by an acquaintanceship. Sometimes it can be a relief just to chat about something trivial or lighthearted without any sense of obligation. If you have a lot on your mind, it may be a welcome change to seek refuge in undemanding social chat. With a friend, you might feel that you had to be more forthcoming, and the friend might be more probing or expect a greater level of interest and curiosity from you.

## Developing a friendship

Often, an acquaintance is someone with whom you have one particular thing in common. You may well have met originally because of this: perhaps you both have children at the same school, use the same sports club, or have a mutual friend. You may have little else in common. It is possible to know an acquaintance for many years and still not progress to a deeper level of friendship, usually because this suits both of you. Other acquaintances are people you have only met recently: people with whom you haven't had time to develop friendship. There may come a point where you realize that you get on well together or have more in common than you had first thought.

An acquaintance may become a friend but this transition requires longer conversations, allowing you time and space to get to know each other better. Both of you must feel the same way about this. If you want to move the relationship on to the next level—becoming friends—you can initiate contact outside your usual sphere, saying something like, "Would you like to have a coffee?" This allows the other person to keep your contact on the same footing if he prefers, or to encourage it to develop. You will have to be sensitive to signals from other people about whether they want to know you better. It is one of the difficulties, and joys, of friendship that there are no clear-cut rules about how to proceed. That's why you should make a point of being aware of the boundaries and expectations of others.

# FRIENDS BY ASSOCIATION

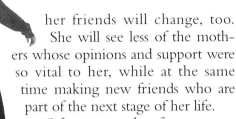

When you look through old photographs, you might occasionally be brought up with a start by the face of a once-close friend who no longer plays a part in your life. You recall both the happy times and the traumas you experienced together. You wonder how you ever came to lose contact with someone you were once so close to, whether it was at college, work, the gym, or the children's playgroup. However, you are unlikely to be filled with remorse, and to berate yourself with, "Oh my God, I should have kept in touch"; you are more likely to remember that, as your circumstances changed, you both realized that you had little else in common and were content to drift apart. You probably feel quite happy to have enjoyed the friendship at the time and have no wish to reestablish contact beyond sending a Christmas card every year.

## Shared experience

Friends you have for a certain period in your life but not forever are called friends by association. Such friendships can be close because they are forged out of a shared experience, such as childrearing, going to college, or working together. It is hard to reconcile the intensity of the friendship then with the distance you feel now, but all this means is that the closeness owed more to the common experience than anything else and that you have both moved on.

It is perfectly natural for friends to pass in and out of your world in this way. At different times in your life you will have different attitudes, interests, and expectations, and your friends will reflect this. A mother with small children is likely to have a number of friends in a similar situation. But when her situation alters as her children start school or she returns to work, it is likely

her friends will change, too. She will see less of the mothers whose opinions and support were so vital to her, while at the same time making new friends who are part of the next stage of her life.

Often people forge new friendships following a divorce or separation. They seek out people in a similar situation, so that they do not feel so isolated. For a while, a friendship between two recently divorced people will be highly valued because each individual knows how the other is feeling and can offer appropriate support and companionship. Yet a few years later, when both have found new partners, they no longer want to stay in touch: the friendship serves only to remind them of a painful period in their lives.

## Support group

Some friendships by association are very brief. Edward, a young executive in his mid-thirties, was chosen by his employers to attend a month-long residential management course. Despite the prestige attached to his selection, Edward spent the long drive to the college moaning to his girlfriend, Ann, about the waste of time and money he thought the course represented. "And besides," he

### Fading friendships
*Some friends feature strongly in our lives for a while, but as the link of a shared experience with them is broken so the friendship quietly fades.*

grumbled, "I won't know anyone there, and they'll all be incredibly boring; it might be bearable if some friends were going too."

For the first week, Ann received nightly calls detailing dull lectures and endless background reading. But by the second week Edward was beginning to sound almost enthusiastic. It became clear that he had developed a rapport with three of the other students and soon Ann was hearing about the nicknames Edward and his new friends had allocated to the other attendees, their struggle to help each other keep up with their studies, and their late-night forays to the local bar.

On his return home, Edward admitted that the course hadn't been so bad after all. He kept in touch with his new friends by phone and finally arranged a weekend reunion. Ann joined Edward to meet the friends and their partners. They had a good time, but Edward knew that the bond the friends had made was already dissolving—the friendships had served their purpose and the friends did not need each other outside the college environment.

## Ever-changing network

Friendships made through shared needs or interests are unlikely to end abruptly. You simply find yourself seeing each other less and less once the common bond has disappeared. One day you notice that someone who has meant a great deal to you no longer plays a major role in your life. You continue to acknowledge him because he once was important to you, but you involve new friends in your current activities.

People appear and disappear from your friendship network in this way all the time. Their path joins with your path for a while and they color your life before branching off again.

# COLLEAGUES

If you go out to work, the majority of your day-to-day relationships are with people you encounter in the workplace. Your place of work is a prime source of friendships of every type. It would be almost impossible not to have some sort of relationship with your colleagues. But just how friendly should you be with them? Should someone in authority fraternize with his or her employees? Should you reveal personal details about yourself to a work friend, or will you be constantly worrying that everybody else knows, too? How can you avoid becoming involved in alliances and feuds, particularly when it is so hard to stay impartial because money and power are involved? And should you steer clear of romance at work, when it is very often its clandestine nature that makes it so attractive?

## Friends and trust
Even if you have good friendships outside work and a warm, loving, intimate relationship, you are still likely to see more of your work colleagues than anyone else, so it is important to try to get on well with them. However, when you start a new job, it is best not to rush in blindly, chatting to everyone as if you've known them for years. It is much better to ease your way in gently and watch how those around you relate to one another. Gradually you will understand the personalities and relationships among your co-workers and learn how to fit in with them. Do not disclose too much personal information at first; wait until you know people well enough to decide whether you can trust them. The last thing you want is to discover that one of your colleagues is spreading intimate details of your life history.

## Dealing with authority
Friendships are generally based on a relationship between two equals. If one person feels superior or inferior to the other, a true friendship will be difficult to maintain. So whether you form friendships with those in authority above you, or those whom you have authority over, depends upon how hierarchical your place of work is. As a boss, it is vital to have the respect of the people who work for you: if you get too friendly with them, this might be difficult to sustain. People in charge have to tread a fine line between appearing approachable and understanding while maintaining a strong sense of fairness, control, and authority. If you form too close a bond with a boss, your co-workers may feel resentful, and you might find yourself in a tricky position if the friendship turns sour.

***Working together***
*Once you have established your position in the work
hierarchy, you can go on to forge rewarding friendships
with your colleagues.*

## Dangerous liaison?

Being thrown together every day, sharing mutual projects, seeing each other at your worst or at your best is quite intoxicating, so it is no wonder that strong bonds are often formed at work. But how far should you go? If you do become romantically involved with a colleague, try to be as discreet as possible. If the relationship develops and your colleagues are aware of what is going on, save the pet names and physical contact for outside work hours. Don't give co-workers the opportunity to cite your romance as a cause of disharmony or reduced work rate. Try to work out what you would do if the romance ended. Could you handle working closely with an ex-lover, or would it be possible to move elsewhere within the company?

## Balancing act

Feuds and alliances are almost inevitable in any setting that involves the daily interaction of people. And sometimes work can be as dramatic as a soap opera: for many people that's what makes it bearable. But becoming too involved in these dramas will be distracting. In order to remain on friendly terms with everyone, you should try to stay neutral: Once you form an alliance in a feud it may be difficult to backtrack and it might not do your reputation any good. If you don't feel you know any of your colleagues well enough to confide in them, and you need to let off steam, discuss the matter with a friend from outside work.

All types of relationships at work demand a tricky balancing act: You want to please yourself, please other people, and make sure that friendships do not adversely affect your professional progress. It can only be good to get on well with your colleagues, even if a friendship doesn't last beyond the confines of a particular job. In some instances, a relationship that you form at work may develop into a strong, close friendship that lasts long after both of you have left your shared workplace.

# CLOSE FRIENDS

**Launching a friendship**
*Although a close friendship will probably have its ups and downs, once embarked upon it could last a lifetime.*

In your friendship network, your close friends undoubtedly take pride of place. These are people you trust the most, care for the most, and need the most. It is unlikely that you will have more than a few close friends, because such valued relationships require enormous input to remain healthy. Close friends are mutually supportive—they know each other well, they appreciate each other's good points and put up with the bad, understanding that all traits contribute to the whole, unique individual. These friends share each other's successes and disasters and remain together through life's turning points.

Both men and women enjoy close friendships with members of their own sex, and although the basic nature of the relationship is the same for both sexes, it is interesting to observe how different the styles of close friendships between men and men and those between women and women actually are.

Women tend to look to their close friendships to provide them with intimate, day-to-day contact, whereas most men prefer to steer clear of personal topics with their close friends unless special circumstances call for it. Some women envy men their ability to form close friendships that do not require them to reveal their innermost thoughts and feelings. And some men envy women the much easier access they have with female friends to candid conversation in which they unashamedly share their fears and their hopes.

## Providing support

Both men and women tell each other their troubles, but they give support in different ways. For example, when Jane was fired from a job she loved, her friend Sophie was extremely sympathetic. She encouraged Jane to talk openly about the hurt she was feeling as well as the anger and sense of betrayal. Sophie told Jane about a time when she, too, had been sacked and how awful she had felt. In this way the two women were able to comfort each other. Sophie felt it important that Jane knew her experience wasn't unique: Sophie had had the same terrible blow. So the women felt they were

### Pulling together

*In times of crisis, close friends should always be there for one another to help each other out of difficulty.*

on equal terms. This reduced Jane's sense of shame, and freed her to be open and honest with her friend.

When Jane's brother Derek was made redundant, however, and he told his friend Bill all about it, Bill's immediate response was to try to help Derek find another job. He did not offer a sympathetic shoulder as Sophie had done to Jane because he did not want to embarrass Derek by encouraging him to show his feelings. Instead, he offered practical assistance. He gave support in a way that did not damage his friend's pride and could easily be accepted gratefully.

So the sexes are subtly different in the way they relate to their own sex. In her bestselling books *You Just Don't Understand* and *That's Not What I Meant!*, Deborah Tannen, Professor of Linguistics at Georgetown University in Washington, D.C., explores some other differences between the ways men and women communicate. Men, she asserts, are much more likely to convey their messages directly; women tend to be indirect.

Men, says Tannen, tend to see themselves in friendships as problem solvers and advice givers, whereas women provide a sympathetic ear and understanding. Men also need to bolster their own image with other men, and they are sensitive about these needs in their friends. They like to impress these friends as a way of maintaining their status. This is why you are far more likely to see a man telling a group of his friends a joke, or performing in some other way, than you are a woman. It is also why Bill's concern was to provide practical help rather than to explore Derek's humiliation.

### Stormy waters

*Close friends have to endure rough times together, as any such relationship will undoubtedly have turbulent moments.*

## Changing situations

Like all relationships, close friendships alter, especially if one of you experiences a major change in your life. Any such change must be understood and accepted by your friend if the friendship is to survive. This may put a huge strain on the relationship; on the other hand, in dealing with that strain it is possible to reinforce the strength and importance of the friendship.

In the case of close friends Paul and Simon, it was the arrival of Paul's first child that put their friendship in jeopardy. Although Simon tried hard to take an interest in the baby, who obviously meant the world to his friend, he found it extremely hard to relate to the new situation and soon became bored with hearing endless details about the child's sleeping habits and milk consumption. Paul saw Simon's lack of interest as a sign of rejection and decided to establish new friendships with like-minded fathers in the area. But Paul soon realized how much he needed his old friend, with whom he had shared so much over the years and who knew him so well. He also discovered that, much as he loved his new role as a father, there were other things he wanted to talk about besides diapers.

Paul phoned Simon and arranged to meet him for a drink. He apologized for the fact that he been preoccupied with his new child, but he warned Simon that exactly the same thing would happen to him if he ever became a father. Simon was delighted to see Paul again. He missed his friend tremendously and had been thinking recently that perhaps he had been selfish in not supporting him through what had obviously been a stressful time. The friendship survived this major change in personal circumstances because both men realized how much they needed each other and weren't too proud to admit it.

## Nurturing friendship

There is no doubt that close friendships are of enormous value. Everyone needs someone to share hopes, fears, successes, and failures with. We learn and grow through our close friendships: very often it is only our closest friends who will be honest with us. Honesty and trust are essential to such relationships. Deceit will be seen as betrayal and will mark the end of the friendship. Always do all that you can to nurture and support your close friendships, whatever the circumstances. Very often they are unique and irreplaceable.

### Cruising along
*Some of the happiest times in our lives will be spent in the company of our closest friends.*

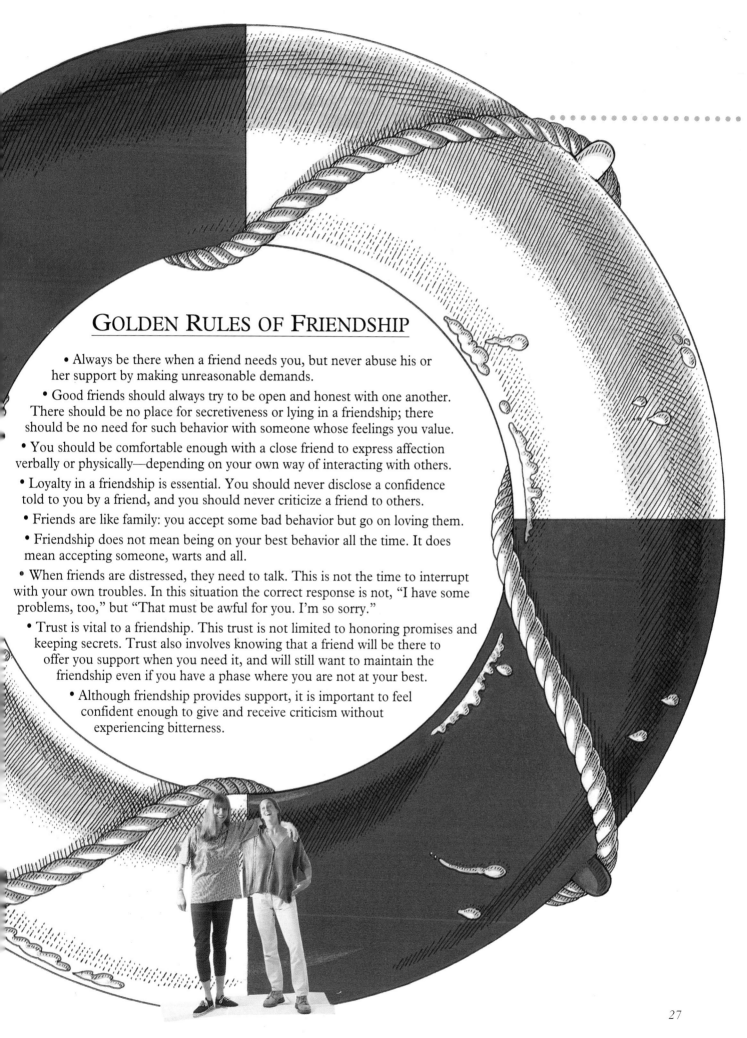

# GOLDEN RULES OF FRIENDSHIP

• Always be there when a friend needs you, but never abuse his or her support by making unreasonable demands.

• Good friends should always try to be open and honest with one another. There should be no place for secretiveness or lying in a friendship; there should be no need for such behavior with someone whose feelings you value.

• You should be comfortable enough with a close friend to express affection verbally or physically—depending on your own way of interacting with others.

• Loyalty in a friendship is essential. You should never disclose a confidence told to you by a friend, and you should never criticize a friend to others.

• Friends are like family: you accept some bad behavior but go on loving them.

• Friendship does not mean being on your best behavior all the time. It does mean accepting someone, warts and all.

• When friends are distressed, they need to talk. This is not the time to interrupt with your own troubles. In this situation the correct response is not, "I have some problems, too," but "That must be awful for you. I'm so sorry."

• Trust is vital to a friendship. This trust is not limited to honoring promises and keeping secrets. Trust also involves knowing that a friend will be there to offer you support when you need it, and will still want to maintain the friendship even if you have a phase where you are not at your best.

• Although friendship provides support, it is important to feel confident enough to give and receive criticism without experiencing bitterness.

# JUST GOOD FRIENDS

WHEN YOU MEET someone of the opposite sex, do you automatically wonder what he or she would be like as a lover? The media bombard us with images of happy couples and exposés of sizzling sexual liaisons, so it is easy to forget that men and women can know each other in any other way. Can men and women be just good friends, or is there a sexual undercurrent inherent in every male-female relationship?

***Platonic partners***
*It is sometimes fun to be with the opposite sex without the demands of a relationship.*

## The joys of the opposite sex

In many cases, a friend's gender seems irrelevant: if you have friends of both sexes, you may not have questioned whether your friendships with each sex differ. But friendships with the opposite sex offer different benefits from same-sex friendships. For example, Peter, a solicitor, finds that his friendships with men tend to be based around work or activities—going fishing, attending jazz concerts, playing poker—but he feels awkward discussing any emotional matters with them. "My mother died recently and my male friends would be very embarrassed if I talked about my feelings openly," he says. "But I have a woman friend who is very supportive and just lets me talk about emotional issues without trying to change the subject."

Having friends of the opposite sex has other benefits, too. It can yield valuable insights into how the other sex thinks, feels, and responds, which also increases your understanding of your partner or of potential partners. Knowing that you are purely friends makes it easier to relax, without the tension of anticipating a possible sexual liaison. If you are an only child or have only siblings of the same sex, having an opposite-sex friend can be like having a brother or sister for the first time. On a practical level, if you are single and are invited to a party or wedding, you may feel more secure and confident if you have an escort, which a good friend can be.

***Increased understanding***
*Having opposite-sex friends provides valuable insights that help you step into each other's shoes mentally.*

## Friendships with ex-lovers

A loving relationship naturally contains a strong element of friendship: perhaps you were initially drawn together by mutual interests or you had many compatible views. If the relationship ends, you may still want to see your ex-partner sometimes. You may well still have a lot in common and there is the advantage that, because your sexual feelings have already been expressed, they are less likely to surface unexpectedly to disturb or even destroy the friendship. There may still be a certain sexual frisson, of course, but it can be easier to contain it harmlessly and confine it to mild flirtation.

## Overcoming obstacles

Not everyone finds it equally easy to relate to the opposite sex in a friendly way. Your background and upbringing inevitably affect how relaxed you feel: you have an advantage if you have one or more siblings of the other sex, if you attended a mixed-sex school, or work with people of both sexes.

For some people, mixed-sex friendships are impossible because of the jealousy of a partner. If your partner feels threatened by relationships of this kind, you may find you avoid them rather than risk a confrontation. Discussing the difficult feelings that are raised is more productive, however: if the problem is not aired, it is likely to resurface later on. Letting each other see opposite-sex friends alone helps build trust in a relationship, and it can be a good harmless outlet for social flirting (see right).

# FLIRTATION

Flirting is one of life's pleasures: How many other things are great fun, cost nothing, and aren't bad for your health? It boosts your self-esteem and confidence, and adds spice to a social occasion. Parties are not the only situations where a little light flirtation can add excitement: discreet, judicious flirting can oil the wheels at a meeting, lighten the atmosphere at an evening class, alleviate a tedious wait at the bus stop or in the supermarket, or relieve the boredom of a dreary day at work.

If you are flirting with someone who is already a friend, there is the advantage that you both know that the flirtation is an enjoyable end in itself, not an invitation to something more. The boundaries are probably already clearly demarcated. On the down side, flirting is all too easily used as a weapon in power games—to make a partner feel jealous, to antagonize a possible rival, to stir up ill-feeling. This kind of provocation is manipulative and destructive. Ask yourself if you ever flirt to "get back" at your partner in some way, or to revel in the feeling of power gained from making someone else hooked on you? In his best-selling analysis of human relations, *Games People Play*, psychiatrist Dr. Eric Berne says some women flirt to arouse a man's interest so that they can reject him once he has shown he is keen. Some men, particularly those with power over women, especially at work, also flirt heavily to seduce a woman, then discard her or even fire her.

Of course, flirting is also a way of showing someone that you are interested in them and would like to know them better. Many relationships start with a flirtatious encounter and this is a highly enjoyable stage for most people: allowing yourself to be slightly risqué, fizzing with the knowledge that greater intimacy will surely follow.

*Confused emotions*
*The art of flirtation needs to be practiced wisely; if misused, it can arouse bad feelings and shake up good friendships.*

## The golden rules of flirting

• **DO** keep it light—humor is a vital tool for successful flirting. Playfulness is more engaging than trying to be a Casanova or a femme fatale.

• **DON'T** flirt with someone you know has a serious crush on you that you don't return.

• **DO** maintain eye contact for just slightly longer than normal. This registers your appreciation of the other person without being too intrusive.

• **DON'T** flirt to score points against your partner or to provoke him or her.

• **DO** be aware of your body language. Angle your body toward the person and mirror his or her posture without being too obvious.

• **DON'T** flirt with someone if you know his or her partner is prone to jealousy.

• **DO** draw attention to yourself by adjusting your hair or clothing slightly: toy with an earring, adjust your scarf or tie, smooth your hair back from your face.

• **DON'T** overdo it. You are out to have fun, not to embarrass yourself in public.

# THE DYNAMICS OF FRIENDSHIP

**A**T ANY SOCIAL GATHERING, different levels of interaction are apparent, varying according to the type and duration of existing relationships, and people's desire and ability to form new friendships. The following party scene may remind you of occasions you have experienced, perhaps when you have had to juggle a conversation between people who had little in common, or smooth over an awkward moment. Looking at the way people's behavior changes will increase your understanding of the dynamics at work between people and the way they shift, altering the responses of individuals and the overall atmosphere.

## Party pieces

Beverly and Robert are giving a housewarming party, and have invited friends, acquaintances, colleagues, and some of their new neighbors. Geraldine, Beverly's best friend since college days, has arrived early to lend a hand; then the two friends take their drinks out into the garden and settle down for a quiet chat. Geraldine has recently split up with her long-term boyfriend, and she wants to talk about it with Beverly.

## Conflicting friendships

While Geraldine is recounting an incident that highlights her mixed feelings about the split, Carolyn—a new friend of Beverly's whom she'd met at work—joins them. Geraldine has already met Carolyn and found her rather superficial. She also feels that Carolyn considers her dull and unstylish, which makes her feel more awkward, so she dries up completely. Carolyn senses that she has interrupted a personal discussion but feels it would be awkward to move away too soon, so she focuses all her attention on Beverly. Carolyn and Beverly are both in the fashion business and Carolyn begins regaling her with a highly amusing account of a glamorous show she has attended, including bitingly accurate impressions of mutual acquaintances.

Beverly is highly entertained but also aware that Geraldine is feeling left out

and upset, so she turns the conversation to a more general subject. Geraldine is still moody and unforthcoming, however, and clearly feels unable to relax with Carolyn there.

At this point, Charles, one of Robert and Beverly's new neighbors, joins the three women with a bottle of wine. As he tops up their glasses, he flirts charmingly with all three of them, then

proceeds to tell them a string of truly terrible jokes that soon has them all laughing in spite of themselves.

## Levels of intimacy

Meanwhile, elsewhere in the garden, Dee, another neighbor, is talking to Graham, who used to play in an amateur softball team with Robert. Robert has found that he no longer has much in common with Graham, so he tends to invite him to occasions where there will be other people rather than seeing him on his own. Graham has been going through a bad patch in his marriage and is talking about this to Dee. She is sympathetic and wants to be helpful, but she also feels a bit awkward because she doesn't really know him.

Charles spots Dee, his neighbor, and comes over. She introduces him to Graham, and Charles,

who is not always very perceptive about atmosphere, happily plunges in and starts talking about local restaurants and places of interest. Initially, both Graham and Dee find Charles rather an intrusion, but his outgoing manner soon has them chatting easily, and Dee starts to feel grateful because she had been finding Graham's confidences a little embarrassing. Graham and Charles then discover they share a passion for sailing and are soon exchanging bits of advice and information, and swapping nautical yarns.

## Finding common ground

Dee feels she cannot contribute to this conversation since she is not interested in sailing, so on the pretext of seeing whether her hosts need any help, she leaves the men and goes into the living-room.

There she finds Beverly and Geraldine talking, so she joins them and is soon deep in conversation with them. Robert comes in to open some more wine; he is keen to get to know his new neighbor, Dee, and becomes involved in the conversation, disagreeing with Geraldine over a question of ethics and being playfully provocative. Feeling relaxed and secure in this company, however, Geraldine is able to rise to the challenge, and argues her point of view clearly but vehemently.

Beverly goes back out into the garden to top up people's glasses. She introduces Carolyn to Charles and Graham and they start talking about their pet hates and then move on to comparing their opinions on the latest books, movies, and television documentaries. Beverly returns to the house where she rejoins the others, who are now engaged in animated discussion.

### Playing your part
*The roles you play vary according to the situation you are in and the people you are with. Some people make it easy for you to be yourself; others make you feel you are having to act a part.*

# NEGATIVE FEELINGS

YOU CAN PROBABLY RECALL one or two occasions when you reacted to a friend's good fortune or happiness with feelings that ranged from discomfort to seething envy. You may feel ashamed to admit to having such feelings toward someone you normally feel so positive about, but all close relationships have some periods of discord as well as periods of harmony.

Many people find that while they can happily discuss personal matters with a friend, they avoid subjects that could lead to disagreement. It can be harder to resolve a conflict with a friend than with a partner: There are more boundaries that you may be wary of breaching and you may feel that a friendship won't be able to sustain the turmoil if you rock the boat. A partner's fundamental feelings for you are expected to keep your relationship afloat even through stormy patches. Often with a friend, there seems to be no way of releasing awkward emotions, such as envy, resentment, anger, or rivalry. However, it is worth finding a way of addressing these difficult feelings: Facing up to them can increase the trust and understanding between you. In addition, it becomes easier to be yourself if you do not have to hide aspects of your character that could cause disagreement.

## Causes of difficulties

Of the many potential causes of conflict in friendships, the following are particularly common:
- **Envy:** This may surface if a friend has something you want or something you feel you ought to have—a well-paid job, a stunning house, etc.
- **Rivalry:** This occurs if you and a friend are both aiming for the same thing, whether it's the same potential partner or a promotion at work.
- **Jealousy:** If a new friend becomes close to one of you, this may be threatening to the other one, who fears being displaced.
- **Resentment:** If you feel a friend has behaved badly and you find it difficult to reproach him or her, resentment is likely to build up. You may expect your friend

to know that he or she has done wrong and to redress the wrong without having to say anything.

• **Differing views:** It is not necessary for friends to agree on every issue. You should be able to agree to differ in many cases, although if the difference is on a fundamental moral, political, or personal issue, it may spell the end of the friendship.

• **Disloyalty:** If a friend is not supportive when you are in need, or if a friend does not defend you against criticism, the behavior may undermine your trust in the other person.

## Facing up to the problem

One issue that may drive a wedge between you and your friend is when one becomes a parent: This may arouse envy or a deep-seated worry that the friend will no longer have time for you, although you may feel ashamed to admit to being jealous of an unborn baby. For example, Julie, an accountant, was 36, recently married, and very much wanted to have a baby. When she hadn't conceived after several months, she and her husband Sam took tests,

### Bridging the gap

*Sometimes it can seem as though there is an unbridgeable gap between you and a friend—an issue that you can neither confront nor ignore—but if you both care about the friendship, you can find a way to cross the gap.*

which revealed that there was a problem but that the couple might be suitable candidates for *in vitro* fertilization. On the same day as the test results came through, Julie's friend Tessa rang in great excitement to tell her that she was pregnant. Their friendship went back to childhood and they were very close. Tessa had only been with her partner for four months and had found it difficult to form a stable relationship in the past. Julie knew that Tessa had been as preoccupied with wanting a baby as she was and that she had started to despair of becoming a mother. However, although Julie tried to be pleased for her friend, she felt as though she had been stabbed in the heart.

As each week passed, Julie's feelings grew more intense. She found it agonizing to hear about Tessa's physical symptoms and the list of possible names she was constantly revising. Too ashamed to admit how she felt, Julie suffered in silence. Eventually, her pain and envy grew too strong, and she started not to return Tessa's calls and began making excuses not to see her. Tessa suspected how Julie was feeling and, while sympathetic, she was also angry and disappointed that Julie couldn't put her own frustration on one side and share her joy.

## Finding a solution

Although Julie and Tessa had had occasional rows in the past, they had been through a lot together—relationship troubles, job crises, money worries—and they had always felt that they were on the same side, secure in each other's support. Tessa didn't want to lose Julie's friendship, but she realized she would have to make the first move. She knew Julie would be evasive on the phone, so she turned up on her doorstep one Sunday evening.

"You're my closest friend," she told Julie. "Having a baby is the most important thing that's ever happened to me and I can't bear for you not to be a part of it. I know how painful all this must be for you, but this baby will need you, too. It needs an auntie. Who else will it turn to when it's annoyed with its parents?" Julie laughed and the two were soon talking again. Julie was pleased that Tessa had shown that she was still valued and needed, and she welcomed the chance to talk to someone besides Sam about her worries regarding fertility treatment.

# DEALING WITH DISCORD

Most of us often find it easier to avoid tackling issues we feel disgruntled or angry about; sometimes we may even feel apprehensive just thinking about telling a friend that he or she has made us angry or hurt. One common way of dealing with discord is to give vent to your feelings by complaining about the friend to another friend or to your partner. Another is to drop veiled hints at the friend in the hope that he or she will understand and will raise the subject or apologize. Perhaps the most common course of action, however, is to say and do nothing in the hope that eventually the problem will sort itself out and that your feelings will evaporate.

### Tending your friendships

*Often the best friendships rely on the willingness of both friends to keep the relationship in good repair, by resolving areas of conflict rather than letting them erode the friendship.*

## Airing your grievances

Unfortunately, none of these approaches really tackles the problem, and all can ultimately lead to a stockpile of unspoken grievances and misunderstandings that erode the strength and warmth of the friendship. Emotional problems have greater destructive power if they are not brought out into the open. You can defuse negative feelings considerably by discussing them. This needn't become a lengthy, soul-searching exercise. Sometimes it is simply a question of raising the issue fairly casually: "You know, I'm genuinely pleased for you that you got your promotion. You worked really hard and you earned it. But—and I'm very embarrassed about this—I've also been feeling envious. I can't seem to make any progress at work and your promotion has made me even more aware of my own frustration." This kind of acknowledgment of the problem not only clears the air—it also leads to a constructive discussion, and even yields positive and helpful suggestions.

In some cases, the problem may be more personal, or it may involve criticizing a friend who has hurt or offended you. Again, expressing your feelings will help, but be careful to confine your comments to the action or event under discussion; if you make a general character assassination, your friend is likely to go on the defensive or march off. Don't say something like: "You never support me in an argument even when you agree with me." Instead, say: "I felt very let down when you didn't back me up. I thought you agreed with me. Is there some reason why you kept quiet?" This approach is much more likely to prompt a positive response.

## Building accord

You don't have to plan your approach as if it were a military campaign, but it is wise to spend some time thinking about exactly what you want to say, and where and when would be best to say it.

**1.** Choose a time when there are just the two of you, and pick a quiet location.

**2.** Keep calm; try not to raise your voice or the talk may develop into a shouting match.

**3.** Be specific—stick to the point. Don't try to deal with every little thing that's ever irritated you over the past decade: focus on the particular issue that has made a discussion necessary.

**4.** Let your friend respond and present his or her point of view without interruption.

**5.** End on a positive note: "We've always been such good friends that I didn't just want to sit and seethe. I really like it that I can be myself when I'm with you—but that includes broaching problems that upset me. I hope you don't feel got at. If I liked you less, I wouldn't have made an effort to sort this out."

Communication is the key to making all relationships work. Talking together will help you understand what is really going on, instead of guessing what the other person is thinking and feeling. Discussing feelings in your friendships, and dealing with conflict as well as joy, will strengthen and enhance your relationships, not diminish them.

# YOUR FRIENDSHIP PREFERENCES

IN OUR SOCIETY a successful life is judged, not only by status, wealth, and professional achievement, but also by how many friends you have. The rich recluse who barricades himself behind electronic gates to avoid human contact arouses not so much envy as pity and incomprehension. Each of us has different friendship needs and preferences: Some people have a very wide circle of acquaintances but no close friends, for example, while others feel happier with a few intimate friends with whom they can forge strong bonds. Your friendships say a lot about who you are and what you think about yourself and other people. What's more, they help to form your sense of identity and your view of the world.

---

*Join hands in friendship*
*Friendships vary from person to person, and alter during our lives. Do you enjoy the casual company of many people, the bonds of a close-knit circle, or a shared intimacy with a few friends?*

---

## What sort of friends do you make?

This questionnaire helps you identify which kinds of contact you tend to form. Read the statements in each category, marking the one that most reflects your view.

### Meeting new people
**a)** I find meeting new people really exciting.
**b)** I am not interested in people with very different lifestyles.
**c)** I usually back away from people who ask me personal questions.
**d)** I can't have a meaningful exchange with someone I've only just met.

### First impressions
**a)** I withhold judgment because I feel everyone's got something to offer if you give them a chance.
**b)** I can tell if somebody's my type at a glance.
**c)** I steer clear of anyone who looks as though they've got a sob story to tell.
**d)** I can usually tell if somebody is sensitive or not.

### Style of communication
**a)** I am at ease in most social situations and have no trouble striking up a conversation with a stranger.
**b)** I find it impossible to communicate with those who have very different interests and views.
**c)** I prefer to talk about impersonal issues rather than personal ones.
**d)** I can communicate freely only with people I know well and trust completely.

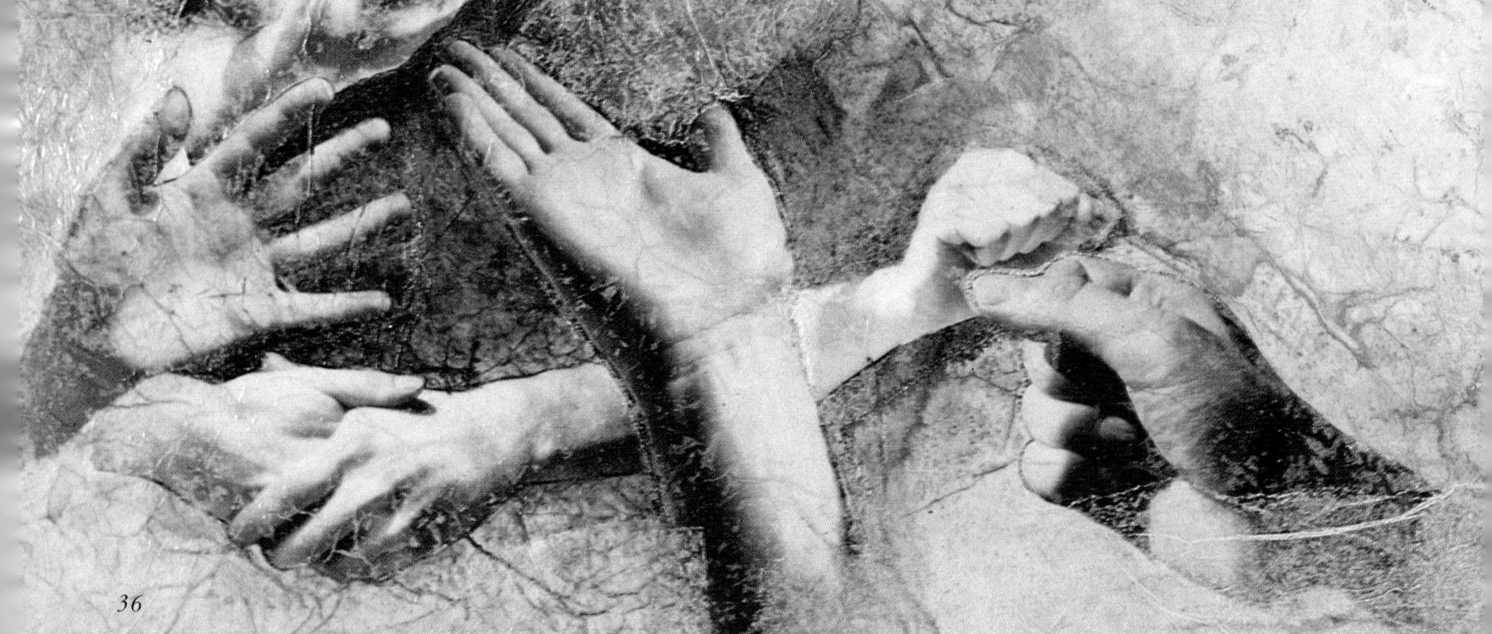

## Work

**a)** I like my colleagues and get on well with them.
**b)** I am friendly with those who think as I do.
**c)** I get on well with my colleagues professionally but have no particularly close work friends.
**d)** I am close to one colleague and we often discuss our problems over lunch.

## Neighbors

**a)** I am happy to chat with most of my neighbors.
**b)** I socialize with those neighbors whose lifestyle is similar to mine.
**c)** I am civil to my neighbors but I wouldn't ask them in for a coffee.
**d)** I am friendly with those neighbors I have come to know well.

## Race and culture

**a)** I am fascinated by people from a different culture or background than my own.
**b)** I don't believe real friendships are possible across an ethnic and cultural divide.
**c)** I get along with any nationality as long as there are things we enjoy doing together.
**d)** Openness and sincerity overcome most barriers.

## Ideal evening

**a)** A big celebration with lots of people or a large dinner party made up mostly of new faces.
**b)** A garden party for professional associates and close members of my social set.
**c)** Clubbing all night with fun people.
**d)** Having a heart-to-heart over a bottle of wine with a close friend.

## Ideal holiday

**a)** Sharing a Mediterranean villa with a mixture of old and new friends.
**b)** A trip to Florence with companions who share my love of food and art.
**c)** An action holiday such as skiing or scuba diving.
**d)** Two weeks in a remote spot with a soul mate.

## Worst nightmare

**a)** Being marooned on a desert island.
**b)** Being kidnapped by aliens from another planet.
**c)** Attending an existential soul-searching session.
**d)** Being conscripted into the army.

# HOW TO SCORE

If you've scored mostly **a**, you come under the category of **People person**, mostly **b** the **Reaffirmer**, mostly **c** the **Non-intimate**, mostly **d** the **Empathizer**.

## People person

You are one of those lucky individuals with a genuine interest in your fellow beings. You can relate to people across the board and your sympathetic approach brings out the best in them. Your large circle of friends includes those whom you have fun with and those with whom you are able to discuss more serious and personal matters.

## Reaffirmer

You tend to seek friendships that confirm your view of yourself and of life generally. You socialize with those who belong to the same social or economic class, who mirror your talents and achievements, or who are part of your professional world. Although you form close and meaningful relationships, problems arise if your circumstances change.

## Non-intimate

You are good fun and probably have a lively circle of friends, but you tend to shy away from intimacy because it makes you feel vulnerable. The fact that you find it difficult to talk about your feelings means that in times of trouble you could find yourself facing them on your own, and your friends might well be unaware of your need for support. Men are more likely than women to fall into this category.

## Empathizer

You are a person who invests a great deal in relationships and one really good friend satisfies your needs. You will open your heart to someone you trust and in return you give every support when they hit a crisis. If a friendship should fail, however, you risk being so devastated that you find it hard to trust again.

# CHAPTER TWO

# LOVE
# MATTERS

HAS THE CONCEPT OF LOVE remained the same throughout the ages or are our twentieth-century expectations of love completely different from those of our ancestors? Chapter Two starts by examining the nature of love. For some, it is a romantic ideal based on the optimistic concept that each of us has a soul mate who will make our lives complete in every way—the search for love is then simply a matter of seeking out that unique individual. For other individuals, love is a much more plannable exercise—it is a search for a life partner who is understanding, loving and as near to an ideal as is reasonable to hope for. Because everybody's experience of love is often quite different, expectations of a relationship can vary enormously from person to person. The "Are You Love Smart?" quiz on pages 48-49 assesses whether you have a realistic expectation of love or not.

The chapter continues by looking at the different kinds of loving relationship and, more particularly, at the specific elements in a relationship that help to make it work. Scenarios describing several different kinds of couple and how their relationships operate prompt you to discover the kind of partner you are

seeking, and what your basic wants and fears really are. Successful relationships are built largely on realistic expectations—of both love and of your partner—and on mutual compatibility. Find out just how well you and your partner are suited to each other by completing the "Are You Compatible?" questionnaire on pages 56-57.

While many people do manage to develop fulfilling relationships, some find themselves in unhappy unions time and time again. This chapter allows you to take a look at the various sorts of love relationship that you get into, and the reasons you choose the partners you do. It shows you how to create a profile of past partners so that you can look at where things tend to go wrong, and then put them right.

Most of the problems people have forming and developing successful relationships stem from childhood impressions. Your attitudes to your partner may well be strongly, but unwittingly, influenced by the manifestations of affection you witnessed during your childhood. This chapter highlights the possible causes of relationship difficulties and offers practical advice on how to change recurring patterns.

BY REVEALING AND EXAMINING YOUR ATTITUDES TO MATTERS OF
THE HEART, YOU WILL LEARN HOW REALISTIC YOUR
EXPECTATIONS OF LOVE REALLY ARE.

# WHAT IS LOVE?

SOME OF THE BEST brains throughout history have tried to define love, including many modern psychologists and sociologists. Good writers, including songwriters, come closest to capturing what it feels like, but not why or how it occurs.

While psychologists have identified many of love's components and attempts have been made to categorize the various kinds of love, its essence remains a mystery. Indeed, attempts to explain it can even deepen the mystery. One definition of romantic love arrived at by a convention of psychologists serves only to confuse: "The cognitive-effective state characterized by intrusive or obsessive fantasizing concerning reciprocity of amorant and feeling by the object of the amorance." Thousands of hours have been spent by psychologists proving that physically attractive people have more success, that we are more attracted to people who show they like us and agree with us, and so on. But while this is probably self-evident to even the most unobservant student of human nature, it doesn't explain why love strikes with one person and not another.

## Love characteristics

We all know what we mean by love. The trouble is that it means different things to different people. One study asked 141 students to list characteristics they associated with the word. They came up with 183 characteristics, of which 115 were mentioned only by one person.

Nevertheless, there is one thing all of us agree on: There is the love we feel for family, children, and friends; and then there is a different kind of love, characterized by romantic and sexual feelings, that we feel when we are involved in an intimate relationship.

Nowadays, before we define ourselves as being "in love," we believe we must "fall" into it—and the kind

### Old romances

*We may dismiss popular ideas of romantic love from fiction and folklore, but their underlying messages—that men are rescuers, women are passive, for example—can still affect our expectations about relationships.*

of love we fall into is romantic. There is nothing new about these intensely romantic feelings, which are usually combined with strong sexual attraction. There is a measurable physiological response: The heart beats faster in the presence of the loved one and there is a light-headed sense of wonderment. A person in love actually looks different: energized, with glowing skin and eyes. Indeed, it is a process so similar to intoxication that experts have compared it to being under the influence of drink or drugs.

Unlike artificially induced euphoria, however, the initial, giddy thrill of falling in love can last for many months—even for as long as two years. While these feelings are probably as old as humankind, it is only in more recent times and in Western culture that this condition has been so exalted. It is usually considered essential to the success of an established relationship that a couple should first be "madly" in love.

## The realities of romance

People sometimes talk of the "history" of love, when what they really mean is the history of the attitudes to love. If you look at history, and the point of view of other cultures with respect to romantic love, you will see that never before recent times and in Western society has it been considered a reliable indication of compatibility, or a prerequisite to marriage.

Historians trace the glorification of romantic love back to the troubadours at the court of Eleanor of Aquitaine in the twelfth century. There, it was unconsummated passion for a married woman, a "courtly love" that expressed itself in devoted idealization of the object. Then, and for many centuries, marriage was something quite different: People married for practical reasons, bearing in mind questions of status. They often grew to love their partners, but they were not "in love." Romantic love as a forerunner to marriage became more generally accepted in eighteenth-century U.S.A. and Europe. It is in the present century, however, that it has assumed the greatest importance.

The difference nowadays is that these heady, wonderful feelings are often perceived as "true" love. This is partly because romantic love is glorified in popular culture. Songs, films, and books concentrate on this early intense phase because it is

*Layers of love*
*You may have to pass through many different emotional stages before you establish a good and loving relationship.*

more interesting to depict than mature love, which is considered ordinary and less thrilling. This wouldn't matter, except that the heightened feelings tend to distort perceptions. You don't notice or mind your loved one's faults, and you behave differently, too—presenting your best side. Under these circumstances, it is hard to be realistic about the potential of a relationship.

If you believe that this ardor is what love is all about, then you will feel profoundly disappointed when the feelings become less powerful, which they inevitably do. At the same time, when the intensity fades, all those faults you ignored become magnified, sometimes leading to an irrational new evaluation of your loved one as fatally flawed. Sometimes a potentially good relationship breaks up at this point.

## TYPES OF LOVE

Some psychologists have defined six types of love experience. These are collaborative love (in which you support each other); active love (in which you do things together); intuitive love (in which you communicate feelings without words); committed love (which supports togetherness); traditional romantic love (which means feeling good); and expressive love (talking about feelings).

Other psychologists suggest a different division, with names taken from Greek and Latin: Eros, or romance and perfection; Ludus, or fun and flirting; Storge, based on friendship; Pragma, based on practical considerations; Mania, which is jealous, obsessive, and possessive; and Agape, which is compassionate and unselfish.

## Courtship

Formalized courtship is a thing of the past, although it still lingers on in some cultures. Nevertheless, the word is still used to describe the process whereby a couple who are in love deepen their relationship with an eye to making it permanent. Sometimes it is accompanied by an engagement. It is the getting-to-know-you phase, when couples talk more intimately about themselves and their plans for the future. It is also a time when the pair introduce each other to family and friends, and are accepted as a couple. When the partners are genuinely compatible, and have more in common than shared passion, the time of courtship can act as a bridge between the intense fervor of romance and the deeper love that marks an enduring relationship. As differences or disappointments emerge, they can learn to accept them while remaining motivated by the fire of romantic love.

One study of dating couples in love asked them to rate their relationships according to the strength of their feelings and also according to how much time they spent doing things together. In the follow-up some months later, it was found that strength of feeling was not a reliable guide to endurance: couples who reported spending a lot of time in joint pursuits were significantly more likely to sustain their relationship.

## Committed love

Sharing activities is one of the main elements that distinguishes committed love from romantic love. Relationships that survive, and perhaps become marriages, need more than passion. Love that endures must also include components more characteristic of friendship, such as respect and admiration. Once couples build a life together,

### Working together

*Happy, successful relationships grow from the willingness of both partners to pull together and share responsibilities as well as pleasures.*

other considerations may dominate their attention and more long-lasting bonds are formed, making romantic love seem less central to their existence.

## Perspective on love

Partnerships can and do survive perfectly well without love, but most people would not want this. The range of loving emotions, from intense passion to gentle affection, is one of life's great pleasures. But all relationships can benefit from understanding that while love smooths the path and is deeply satisfying, it is not the only ingredient to be found in successful unions.

Falling in love is marvellous, but remember that it is possible to feel very passionately about someone who is actually profoundly unsuitable for you. Equally, you should not assume that the natural quietening of passionate love indicates that the relationship is dying.

Loving someone gives you the impetus to ride over the rough patches that affect every relationship, but love alone won't cure problems. Tolerance, humor, understanding, and compromise are more important, in the end, than the intensity of the love that you feel. The bonus is that dealing successfully with the everyday niggles or major crises that are bound to happen over the years deepens love. And while the heady rapture of early passion always subsides, many couples continue to feel romantic about each other.

The difference is that mature romance is no longer a spontaneous result of simply being in each other's company. Instead it becomes a more conscious expression of generosity and warmth. Romance grounded in affection, mutual interests, and shared experience is enduring, and it can make you feel happier and more special than the less stable accident of first love.

## LOVE AT FIRST SIGHT

Love at first sight is often considered to be a myth, but too many people have experienced overwhelming and instantaneous passion at first meeting for it to be dismissed so lightly. But can it be trusted? Can a feeling that strikes so quickly and suddenly really be a sound basis for a lasting relationship?

Psychological experiments have shown that we have an uncanny ability at first meeting to gravitate toward people who have many psychological and developmental similarities to ourselves. Add the still little-understood element of sexual attraction, and you have all the ingredients of love at first sight. Of course, instant passion can evaporate quickly, but many couples enjoy an enduring partnership that began this way.

*Bolt from the blue*
*For some couples, the initial lightning strike of attraction develops into a lasting and rewarding relationship.*

The success of such relationships hinges partly on whether the emotional attraction beneath the physical one is healthy: some people are compulsively drawn to those who will hurt them. Essentially, love at first sight is the most dramatic type of romantic love; its survival, therefore, depends on the couple's compatibility and willingness to work at the relationship once the romantic stage has passed.

# ARE YOU A LOVE JUNKY?

When you're attracted to someone new, do you feel exhilarated and on top of the world, bursting with life and vitality? Does this happen again and again? If so, you could be a love junky. For some people, the experience of falling in love is so central to life, even to the extent that it validates their existence, that they become addicted to it. They get hooked on the euphoric fix of that first blaze of passion and even when their relationships consistently turn sour, they go after the same feelings over and over again. To love junkies, it is only true love if it includes intense highs and lows, the heady rush of adrenaline, feelings of butterflies in the stomach; if these people are not teetering on an emotional cliff-edge, it isn't love.

The problem that love junkies face, however, is that they become incapable of sustaining a long-term, committed relationship. They yearn for the closeness and genuine intimacy of healthy affection but have never achieved it and don't know how to develop it. In their experience, love crashes in wildly rather than growing gradually. They don't know how to choose a suitable love partner for a long-term relationship and have no experience of allowing love to develop at its own pace.

## Questionnaire

The following questions, which focus on different aspects of love, will help you find out whether you are a love junky. Answer Usually, Sometimes, or Never; then turn to page 138 for the analysis.

**1.** Do you feel an instant and irresistible sexual attraction to your partners?
**2.** When someone makes a strong play for you, does that make you fall for him or her?
**3.** Do you start each new relationship feeling that this time you may achieve perfection?
**4.** Do you feel most alive when you are experiencing the highs and lows of an intense relationship?
**5.** Do you enjoy being swept off your feet by a stranger?
**6.** Do you feel that your love relationship should put all other areas of your life into the shade?
**7.** Do you find that once your passion fizzles out you get bored?
**8.** Do you repeatedly become disillusioned with your partner and look around for someone else?
**9.** Do you usually believe that things will work out with your next partner?
**10.** Do you experience the same emotions with a new partner as with all the previous ones?

# WHEN ROMANTIC LOVE STOPS

Whether you are a love junky or not, like most people you will inevitably find that the first blaze of passion in your relationship dies down. You may imagine that the relationship is dying, too, that the connection between you and your partner is breaking. In fact, it probably means that the relationship has switched into another phase—one where emotional intimacy is more important than sexual intimacy, where the gentle comforts of being together outweigh the passion. This phase is more realistic and enduring than heart-stopping lust. This is a normal part of a healthy relationship, but both partners need to be prepared to adjust to these changes to keep their affection alive.

If you find that your contentment becomes complacency, that you start to take your partner for granted or to lose interest, try following some of these tips:
• Be honest with yourself and your partner, and work together to deepen your relationship and improve it as you need to.
• Your sex life doesn't have to be daring or adventurous, but it's a good idea not to let it become too routine; for ideas, see "When the Chemistry Changes," pages 136-37.
• Accept your need for novelty and, together, look at areas where you find your relationship boring or stale so you can work on changing those areas.
• Find new things to do together: vacations, evening classes, joining a sports club, taking up photography.

*On the right track*
*When it feels as though the romantic phase of your relationship has come to an end, you can move onto a new track—one of deeper emotional intimacy.*

• Understand that there is room in your relationship for other people, and enjoy their company.
• Don't expect to be everything to each other: you have separate needs for time on your own and for your own interests, as well as for time with your family and friends.
• Don't let routine dominate your life—predictability can easily deaden your emotions.
• Keep communicating—about yourselves, the relationship, and outside interests. Relationships die if you have nothing to say to each other.
• Be prepared for your relationship to keep changing; be ready to keep realigning the things you do together; see "Managing Change," pages 104-105.

*Bittersweet love*
*Like eating too much candy, getting hooked on the sensation of falling in love may yield a short-term high but is ultimately bad for you.*

# TYPES OF RELATIONSHIP

As you grow up, you want different things from life: As a child, you may want no more than the chance to stay up late or to eat sweets all day; later on, you may long to do well in your exams or to get a date with the school heartthrob; as an adult, your thoughts may focus on fulfilling your potential in your profession or on creating a happy environment for your children. Similarly, the type of relationship you want will probably change during your life: when you are a teenager starting to have dates, you are looking for a different kind of relationship from the one that will suit you when you want to have children.

Up until around your mid-twenties, romance may be high on your list of priorities. After that, you may begin to consider settling down, so commitment and stability assume greater importance. Later on in life, the companionable elements of a relationship can assume more importance. This is a generalization, of course, and many people want passion right through life, or look for commitment or companionship very early.

Some lucky couples meet and marry their first love, and their relationship adapts through the years to their changing needs and circumstances. It is not uncommon nowadays, however, to have a series of relationships—at least during the first half of your life—each serious and important in its own way.

### Know your needs
*For some young couples, fun and passion may be more important needs than stability and commitment.*

## Meeting your needs

Whichever stage of life you are in, knowing what you want from a relationship helps you in choosing a partner. If you are out of synch with your partner —one of you wants security or children, and the other just wants fun—there will be problems between you, however well you get along. Sometimes it is precisely because you don't talk about what you are really looking for from the relationship that unnecessary difficulties are created.

Realizing that a relationship that suited you once now no longer meets your needs will always be problematic. Do you try to change the nature of your existing relationship, or do you look for someone else? When you are not married and there are no children involved, you might well decide to end it. The more enmeshed your lives become, with home, family, friends, and finances in common, however, the harder it is to do this. Many people do part—as the divorce figures testify—but others try to find an alternative solution. Some embark on a series of affairs, hoping to siphon off the tension in the marriage by having a new focus. A few do this openly, with all the people involved being aware of the situation.

In a way, this is the uneasy Western version of polygamy, or the practice of having multiple partners, which is a long-established tradition in some cultures. More usually, a man in these societies takes a number of wives, depending on his ability to provide for them all, although in some cases a woman can take more than one husband. All the spouses in these set-ups are legitimate and become part of the same family, often having defined roles according to hierarchy and age. The children are all cared for in an active extended family.

The modern equivalent in our society is that the partners have affairs, or divorce and remarry. This, by contrast, creates less stability. The lovers or the divorced partners have little status or security, and the children from affairs or broken marriages often lose out, emotionally or financially.

## High expectations

The causes of accelerating relationship breakdown are numerous. Divorce no longer carries the stigma it once did. People move around more, and often do not have a close framework of family and

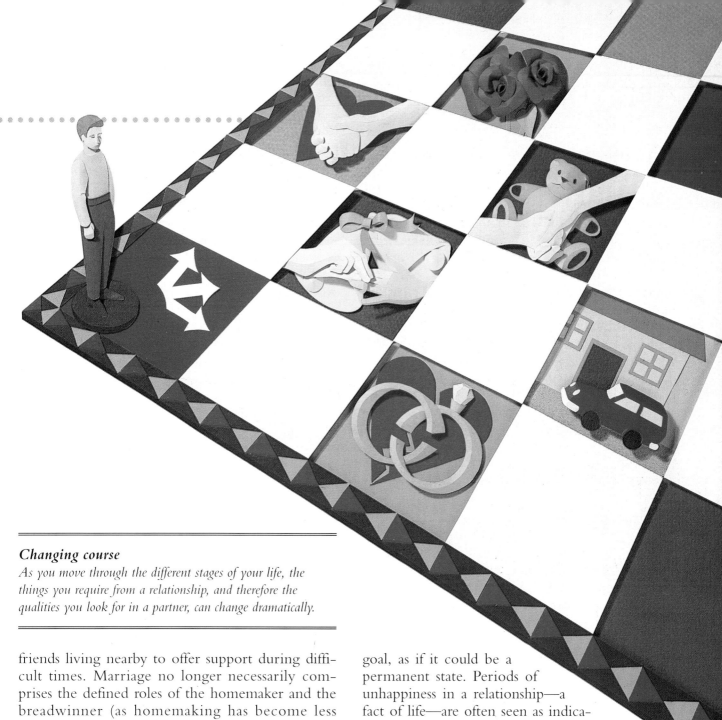

## Changing course

*As you move through the different stages of your life, the things you require from a relationship, and therefore the qualities you look for in a partner, can change dramatically.*

friends living nearby to offer support during difficult times. Marriage no longer necessarily comprises the defined roles of the homemaker and the breadwinner (as homemaking has become less time-consuming and labor-intensive); these mutually dependent roles provided a structure that was more important than the individuals' happiness. Also, the average life expectancy has increased, so while in the past marriages were cut short by death, nowadays, they can be expected to last for 30 or 40 years or more. Less tangible, although equally potent, is that in our society there is really only one type of accepted relationship: the exclusive, intense partnership in which partners look to one another to provide all their emotional needs—support, friendship, passion, and happiness.

These expectations put a great strain on even the best relationships. Although happiness is something that comes and goes, many people aspire to it as a goal, as if it could be a permanent state. Periods of unhappiness in a relationship—a fact of life—are often seen as indications that the relationship itself is wrong.

## Contentment by contract

The causes of relationship breakdown might be obvious, but the solutions are less clear. Some advocate fixed-term contracts for marriages, in which the couple commit themselves to stay together at least during their children's formative years, come what may. These could then be re-negotiated for a longer period should all go well.

As relationships stand now, however, the onus is on individual couples to work out their own solutions, bearing in mind the well-being of all involved. It is a creative challenge—one that can offer some of the greatest rewards in life.

# Are You Love Smart?

Do you believe that love is all you need to sustain a happy relationship, or do you understand that you have to work at it, too, but are not quite sure what this means? In all sorts of relationships, whether a long-term marriage or a brief affair of passion, there are common elements that lead to success. Many relationships founder because partners do not have realistic expectations—of themselves, of each other, or of what the relationship can provide.

Successful relationships depend on communication, compatibility, realism, and being thoughtful and considerate toward your partner. The following questionnaire will help you assess your attitudes to relationships. Read each statement and consider how accurately it sums up your feelings about love, now or in the past. Decide whether it applies to you very much, quite a lot, not very much, or not at all; then check your score, far right. If you are love smart, this doesn't necessarily mean that you will quite naturally forge successful relationships with every potential partner you meet; similarly, if you are not particularly love smart, you are not necessarily condemned to a string of failed relationships. Responding honestly to the statements can help you learn whether your attitudes and actions are sabotaging your efforts at establishing a successful relationship.

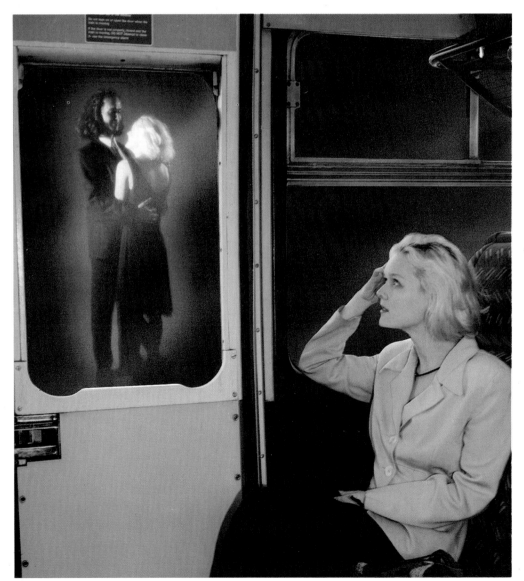

**Damaging dream**
*Daydreaming about a fantasy romance may seem harmless, but if it prevents you from forming an imperfect but real relationship, it will spoil your chances of being happy and fulfilled.*

**1.** Partners who are truly in love spend all their time together.

**2.** Telling my partner that I love him or her will make up for the times I treat him or her badly.

**3.** Opposites attract: I want a partner quite different from myself.

**4.** If somebody is attracted to me, I'm willing to start a relationship.

**5.** If my partner has a personality trait that I don't like, I can change it.

**6.** If my partner is right for me, love will carry us through.

**7.** As long as my partner and I have good sex, it means our relationship is going well.

**8.** It worries me when I find myself attracted to people other than my partner.

**9.** If a relationship is working, it is always exciting.

**10.** I can't start to enjoy life until I have a partner.

**11.** I know when a relationship is right by how lovesick I feel.

**12.** My lover and I should always be perfectly in tune with each other.

**13.** When I start a relationship with someone, I have a right to know everything about him or her.

**14.** Because I've been hurt so many times before, I have difficulty trusting my partner.

**15.** If my partner loves me, he or she will always be pleased to see me even if I turn up unexpectedly.

**16.** I like to communicate openly by always saying to my partner exactly what I am feeling.

**17.** I don't necessarily expect to stop seeing other lovers during a relationship.

**18.** I like my partner to take an interest in everything I enjoy doing.

**19.** When I have a close relationship, I stop seeing my friends and family.

**20.** Once I stop feeling weak at the knees, I know a relationship is over.

## Conclusion

Your responses should give you a good idea of how attitudes may impede your ability to maintain good relationships. Examine your past, and see whether you can trace back any of the problems you have experienced to your attitudes. Accepting that you are partly responsible for any difficulties you have had is an important step on the way to creating successful relationships.

## HOW TO SCORE

Give yourself four points every time you responded "very much," three points for every "quite a lot," two points for "not very much," and one point for "not at all." Then add up your score and read the analysis that applies to you.

A score of 60-80 means that you are not love smart at all. Be honest with yourself: are you living in a fantasy, dreaming of the perfect love, while you sabotage your efforts at making a relationship work and give yourself a lot of heartache into the bargain? You need to take a hard look at your attitudes and understand how they could have caused problems in the past. Don't worry: You are not doomed to be mistreated and dumped by every partner who comes along. You can learn to choose partners more wisely and to get on with them better, in a way that will allow the best of each of you to come out.

If you scored 40-59, this means you are not sufficiently love smart: you keep being hurt in relationships and are loath to trust people. You are still convinced, however, that the perfect partner will come along and everything will turn out to be wonderful. You need to be much more realistic about what to expect from love, and make some changes to the way you behave with your partners.

A score of 30-39 means that you are fairly love smart in some areas but still believe in a few unrealistic romantic ideals. Remember that a relationship is a private affair between two ordinary people: you do not need to be perfect, or expect your partner to be perfect either. Try to accept a relationship as part of your life, rather than seeing it as life itself.

If you scored 20-29, you are pretty love smart. You understand that love is not enough to sustain a relationship and you have realistic expectations of love. Look again at the statements that you scored over one point for: they will probably have caused problems in your past and present relationships.

# ARE YOUR EXPECTATIONS TOO HIGH?

At various times in our lives, we all find the world a hard place. Daily life with its trials and challenges is often a struggle. Many of us work, study, socialize, and raise children in an environment that seems harsh, anonymous, and uncaring—particularly when additional personal problems make us feel vulnerable and isolated. In the past, people perhaps accepted this more as a fact of life, pinning their hopes on the promise of paradise in the next world. In this more secular age, however, a dominant idea in Western culture is the belief that the panacea for life's troubles is to be found in the "perfect relationship."

## The perfect relationship

The perfect relationship is, of course, a myth. Of all modern myths, it is possibly the most powerful, promoted by the glamorized visions of movies, pop songs, and romantic fiction. The perfect relationship is one in which the partner supplies everything the other could possibly desire—an almost mystical union of the physical, mental, spiritual, and emotional needs of two individuals. Furthermore, it is expected to provide all these things forever. In a nutshell, the perfect relationship is everything the imperfect—but real—world is not.

***Romance versus reality***
*The idea of the perfect relationship is an alluring mirage, insubstantial and unsatisfying.*

Adherence to this fantasy causes many problems. Indeed, it is often the underlying reason for dissatisfaction with a relationship and the cause of its failure. Many people believe that the heady intoxication of the early "in love" phase is love at its truest. During this period, everything is harmonious and intensely gratifying. Passion runs high and communication seems effortless. The frustrations of life seem insignificant because for one special person the other is the center of the universe.

Letting go of this blissful dream and accepting that high romance is a phase that inevitably ends can be painful. To do so, however, is to take a giant step toward building a genuinely fulfilling and loving relationship.

## Making false assumptions

In order to thrive, all relationships need commitment and effort. Two people who share a life naturally come to expect a whole series of things from one another, both on a practical and an emotional level—and this is how it should be. Things can go wrong, however, if either of you starts to believe that you own your partner in some way. This leads you to demand things that you would not dream of demanding from anybody else.

A common form this assumption takes is to presume that the purpose of your partner's life is to complement yours. Things that from the rest of the world must be earned we expect from a partner as a right. We demand that they show an interest in whatever we are doing, despite the fact that it might be dull or that they have other things on their mind. We demand respect and support at all times, including when it's not deserved. We demand to be loved when at our most unlovable, and to be desired no matter how undesirable we might have become. Because the partner is "ours," we feel that everything is due. This is especially true when it comes to emotional fulfillment. If we are dissatisfied or disappointed—if life is letting us down—it may seem easier to lay the blame squarely at our partner's door. It may be tempting to abandon responsibility for our own happiness and make it his or hers instead.

The idea that one person can provide everything you need is a particularly dangerous aspect of the romantic myth. Everyone has a mixture of strengths

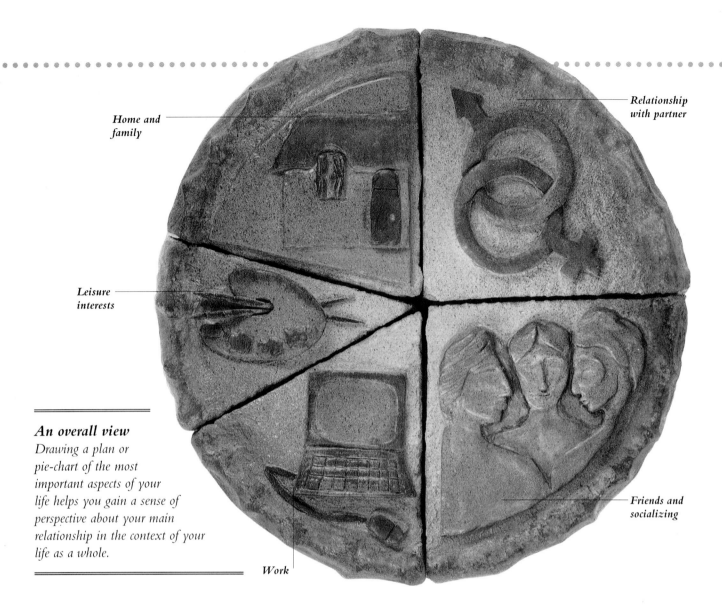

Home and
family

Relationship
with partner

Leisure
interests

Work

Friends and
socializing

**An overall view**
*Drawing a plan or
pie-chart of the most
important aspects of your
life helps you gain a sense of
perspective about your main
relationship in the context of your
life as a whole.*

and weaknesses, and we all grow and change. A woman who marries at 20, for example, will have different requirements five years on, when she's juggling a job with raising children. A young man just starting out on a career will want other things from his partner when his prospects are more established. Furthermore, your needs differ according to circumstance and your mood. You have to accept that while a partner might be wonderfully supportive when you are low, he or she may empathize less with your enthusiastic moments. Your partner might be the ideal person with whom to take a country walk, but not so good at a party.

## Building a balanced life
Your relationship needs to be part of a rounded, well-balanced life—a life that does not focus exclusively on any one area, but includes a range of

elements. In her book *Feel the Fear and Do it Anyway*, American psychologist Susan Jeffers suggests making a "whole-life grid" and dividing it into compartments. In each compartment you write an aspect of your life that is important to you—for example, your relationship, family, friends, work, a leisure activity, time you spend alone, or time you spend doing things for others.

Try this exercise yourself, using a grid or pie-chart to show the elements of your life that matter to you. This will help you to gain a broader perspective on your own life, giving you a kind of bird's-eye view. Putting your relationship into a wider framework does not mean neglecting it; nor does it mean loving your partner any less. It means respecting your own and your partner's individuality and freeing your relationship from unrealistic and unfair expectations.

# MAKE THE RIGHT CHOICE

O F COURSE, you wouldn't set out to choose a partner who will make you unhappy, nor would you deliberately give your heart in a relationship that is bound to fail. Nevertheless, many people have found themselves making choices that are not right for them, or committing themselves wholeheartedly to relationships that go wrong.

It would be wonderful if there was a foolproof formula that you could apply to a potential partner to test the durability, appropriateness, and happiness of a relationship together. Nothing is certain in the field of human relations, however, and even matches between perfectly complementary people sometimes collapse.

What you can do, however, is maximize your chances of choosing well by avoiding pitfalls. The main elements in this are understanding yourself well, getting to know your partner, and assessing the likelihood of your future compatibility. Examining and identifying your attitude to romantic love is the first step.

## The role of romantic love

Falling in love has much to recommend it, but it is not the most reliable predictor of success in a relationship. Fortunate people do find that those they fall in love with turn out to be the very ones who are good, long-term matches for them. Others are less lucky. What romance shows more reliably is that there is probably a strong sexual attraction and mutual good feelings that give a relationship a head start. Many people would never consider making permanent a relationship that did not begin with romantic attraction. The truth is, however, that long-term stability depends on different things. So long as you bear this in mind, you can still enjoy what romance has to offer, without letting it lead you into making unwise decisions.

*Informed choices*
*Be carefully attuned to exactly what it is you are looking for in a partner before you make a choice.*

*A new template*
*Understanding the reasons for past problems makes it easier for you to create a new template for the way in which you approach relationships.*

If you feel that you have been unlucky in love, you will find that it helps to analyze your own romantic inclinations. When lust has always been the main ingredient and you become bored or keen to look elsewhere within a short time, then you know that you have a propensity to fall in love for physical reasons alone. Perhaps in the past you have ignored people who don't immediately attract you across a crowded room. This is a sign that you need to pay attention to less obvious contenders, rather than ruling them out because you are not physically drawn to them straightaway; you will probably find that physical attraction as well as love can grow with a person you find likable and interesting.

Conversely, sex might only be one element in your romantic encounters, yet you are always attracted to people who turn out to be wrong for you. This is why you need to know what makes you tick.

## Understanding yourself

Most of us have quite a good idea of what we are looking for in a relationship, but it is harder to grasp the unconscious motivations that affect the choices we make. Without being aware of it, we are drawn to make matches that somehow echo our early experiences of relationships—the one our parents had with each other, and those we formed with each of them, with siblings and others when we were young. Like it or not, our own relationships appear to reproduce these in some form. This is fine if the role models we had were good, or if we were usually treated well; then our attraction is more likely to be for people with whom we can live together happily and rewardingly.

For one reason or another, however, many people have less-than-golden memories of childhood. Any difficulties between our parents, or unsatisfactory treatment of ourselves, subtly conditions us to "recognize," in a way we experience as attraction, people with whom we form similar kinds of relationships. One theory is that we are actually attracted to relationships that work in a familiar way—even if they make us unhappy. Another is that we make these repetitive relationships because we subconsciously want to put right what went wrong before—and somehow transform the bad into good.

## Repeating past patterns

Many people resist these ideas because they can't believe that any part of them wanted to choose someone who would make them unhappy. They can't see the least correlation between their partners and experiences in the past. Nevertheless, a woman may find herself with a man who is violent just as her father was, or emotionally cold as her mother was; and a man may find himself with a wife who nags or sulks like his mother, or doesn't think he'll amount to much, just as his father believed, and so on.

It might be hard to spot the connection, but if you are aware that you often make the wrong choices, looking back on your own childhood can illuminate possible reasons. If your relationships tend to reinforce old feelings of unworthiness, unhappiness, fear of loss, or other uncomfortable emotions, then you should take this as a message from your subconscious that these are issues you need to resolve—and doing so in a relationship might not be the best way.

There are two main ways of handling such problems. One is to decide to avoid becoming involved with people you are instantly attracted to, but who experience has shown are bad for you. Instead, spend time with people who make you feel good. Curiously, many people who go for the wrong partners often know people who have all the right qualities yet "can't" find them attractive. Giving relationships with these people a chance may be just what you need.

## First impressions

*Don't rely on a superficial impression: take the time to get to know a potential partner well so that you have a good idea of how compatible the two of you are.*

This is hard, however, particularly when it is important for you that a relationship should start with a strong physical attraction. A much more reliable way of avoiding the wrong partners and picking the right ones is to deal with the childhood issues that have caused the problem (see "Feeling Good about Yourself," right). Although this is not easy either, the better you feel about yourself, the more likely you are to choose people who will make you feel good. If you feel unlovable, for instance, it won't seem too unreasonable to fall for people who treat you badly. But if you feel worth more, then you will not find such people attractive.

## Getting to know your partner

One of the illusions of romantic love is that you feel that you know all there is to know about each other. How you make each other feel is what seems most important. This is the best time, however, to talk intensively about yourselves and get to know more than each other's biographical details. Knowing whether you are making the right choice means having a proper understanding of your partner's nature and desires—the bad as well as the good. The bonus is that while you are in love, it is relatively easy to come to terms with each other's less savory characteristics which, of course, everyone has. You can't make a proper, informed choice unless you know your partner very well. What matters then is being able to assess and predict your future compatibility.

## Will it work?

The issues most couples argue about are housework, child-rearing, money, and responsibility. These are the stuff of everyday life, and they are certainly not romantic. Perhaps that is why few people talk about such matters when they are courting and in love—but they loom large later on in a committed relationship. Knowing whether you are compatible or not means being able to discuss these sorts of things before they become central to your life together.

Other issues, of course, also enter the equation. Having a similar outlook and wanting many of the same things in life will help to ensure that you are not clashing about major decisions later on. Compatibility also depends on less tangible elements. Two of the most important are how you both handle the important emotions of love and anger. Does either of you feel awkward about showing or receiving affection? Do you hold your anger in, or let it out in a great explosion of rage? True compatibility often relies more on understanding and accepting each other's modes of expression, difficulties, or needs, than it does on having the same responses.

Most of these and other issues of compatibility depend on getting to know each other gradually. If you make a lifetime decision based on only three months of ecstatic love, therefore, you might never have had the chance to disagree, or ever talked more than sweet nothings to each other. Making the right choice, based on genuine knowledge and understanding, then, needs time. Wrong choices are often the result of decisions made too early, or of a willful ignoring of signs that there is likely to be unhappiness ahead.

## Sustaining the momentum

People's attitudes and modes of behavior are bound to change with time and experience, and circumstances arise that can cause all kinds of difficulties in life generally and in relationships particularly, so lasting compatibility depends on much more than making the right choice in the first place. It requires both an open and flexible attitude and an active commitment from both partners in the relationship. Of course, an unhappy relationship can still result even when you make a good choice of partner. You will have to put the same amount of energy into establishing and maintaining a good relationship that you put into choosing your partner initially.

## FEELING GOOD ABOUT YOURSELF

People who are happy with themselves are less likely to choose partners who treat them badly. Tackling poor self-esteem, fears, and other legacies from the past takes time but pays dividends. The better equipped you are to create happiness for yourself, the less you feel the need to jump into a relationship—any relationship—rather than being alone. You can afford to be choosy.

Treating yourself well is a good first step. If you don't think much of yourself, you are susceptible to anyone who shows you a little attention. Have a good time and build on your existing friendships. Developing confidence is even more useful. If you have put up with bad behavior in the past because you thought your partners were better than you or could do things you couldn't, then discovering your own talents and strengthening your weaknesses protects you for the future. Build on anything you do well—be it a hobby, interest, knack with

people, or skill at work—and congratulate yourself for your successes. Writing them down helps. Real confidence, however, comes from transforming your perceived weaknesses. One by one, tackle what you think you lack: intelligence, driving skills, temper control, decision-making ability, or whatever. If you put determination and time into improving what you dislike or find disappointing about yourself, you may be surprised at the change. The thrill and the assurance that results from succeeding where you used to fail will not only improve what you have to offer partners, but also convince you that you deserve better from them—and therefore have the right to be more selective.

### Strong roots
*Improving your actual skills, as well as your perception of them, strengthens the roots of your self-esteem. Once you value yourself, others are more likely to value you, too.*

# ARE YOU COMPATIBLE?

This two-person questionnaire is designed to help you and your partner assess your compatibility. First answer "yes" or "no" to each question, then let your partner do the quiz on his or her own. Count up the number of times your replies tallied, then look at the solutions on the right.

## Group 1

1. Are your parents still living together?

2. Are you the oldest child in your family?

3. Are you the youngest?

4. Are you somewhere in the middle?

5. Are you an only child?

6. Do you continue to live at home with your parents?

7. Is your family close knit?

8. Do you and your partner come from the same country or ethnic group?

9. Do you share the same religion?

10. Do you and your partner come from the same social background?

11. Do you now move in a different social circle from the one you were brought up in?

12. Do you come from the same town or part of the country?

13. Have you travelled abroad?

14. Did you go on to higher education?

15. Are you in the job of your choice?

## Group 2

1. Do you and your partner share the same sense of humor?

2. Do you agree politically?

3. Do you believe we all have a moral obligation to involve ourselves in wider social issues?

4. Are family values being eroded?

5. Do you think that, when possible, old people should live with their families rather than be put into residential homes?

6. Do you think children are an essential part of a fulfilling relationship?

7. Do you see good parenting as one of life's most important tasks?

### Shared outlook

*During the early stages of a relationship, differences of opinion may seem to be of little consequence. But if you are hoping that your partnership will last, it is useful to discover whether you agree on most issues or if there are any areas where you disagree strongly.*

**8.** Do you think incompatible parents should stay together for the sake of the children?

**9.** Do you think it is acceptable to leave your children in the care of others?

**10.** Do you think a mother should stay at home while her children are young?

**11.** In your opinion, should both partners share domestic chores and child-rearing equally?

**12.** Do you consider a large salary to be more important than job satisfaction?

**13.** Do you think it's more important to save money than splash out on treats?

**14.** Do you think it is beneficial to a relationship that a couple continues to pursue independent hobbies or interests?

**15.** If your partner disliked your closest friends, would you stop seeing them?

## Group 3

**1.** Is a loving relationship the most important thing in your life?

**2.** Is building a successful career your foremost commitment?

**3.** Are you looking for a soul mate to be your "other half"?

**4.** Do you want a partner who will take care of you forever?

**5.** Is the prospect of loneliness one of your greatest fears?

**6.** Are you looking for someone solid and dependable to have children with?

**7.** Do you think that exciting and passionate sex is the key to a long-lasting relationship?

**8.** Would you describe yourself as an essentially extroverted and optimistic person?

**9.** Do you believe expressing anger is positive because it helps to clear the air?

**10.** Do you think that couples are bound to grow apart with the passing of time?

**11.** Do you think it is important for a person to spend time alone regularly?

**12.** Do you believe discussing personal problems only makes them worse?

**13.** Do you think that a couple should always be totally honest with one another, even when the truth might hurt the other person's feelings?

**14.** Do you believe obsessional jealousy between partners is proof of real love?

**15.** Is infidelity something you could never forgive your partner for under any circumstances?

# SOLUTIONS

If 15 or fewer of your answers agreed with those of your partner, then things don't look too bright as far as long-term compatibility is concerned. When the initial, exciting flush is over, it is probable that fundamental differences will surface and begin to make waves. In all likelihood, your relationship will not survive beyond the "in love" phase.

If 16-30 of your answers tallied, you are sufficiently compatible to feel optimistic. By identifying those areas where you are out of step, you can start to deal with potential problems before they get out of hand. How long your relationship lasts will depend on keeping a dialogue open.

If your score was over 30, you are definitely well matched. As well as coming from similar backgrounds, you share the same hopes about what you want from your relationship, and how you envisage family life. The indications are that your partnership will be long and rewarding.

Although there are certain factors that contribute to a compatible and enduring relationship—such as coming from a similar background, sharing race, religion, and social class, etc.—they are not in themselves decisive. If they were, only people who married the boy or girl next door would go on to have happy partnerships. More important elements are your basic personality and the values you have formed about life, love, and relationships. Equally influential is your attitude toward differences. If you listen to your partner's opinions and feelings with respect, and take into account his or her point of view, you can negotiate more effectively those areas on which you contrast. Differences handled this way can be used to create a compatibility of the best kind.

# WORKING RELATIONSHIPS

When two individuals get together their relationship takes on an identity all its own. The character and needs of each individual within a relationship determine how the pair behave toward one another and how they present themselves to others. To help you judge what kind of central love relationship suits you, read the scenarios below, which describe how five successful relationships work, and then answer the questions that follow. These questions should prompt you to define what you need from a relationship. There are no right answers to the questions. The important thing is to use your answers to help you understand whether your relationship is giving you what you need in a healthy and constructive way.

## Scenario 1: Mutual trust

Carrie and Spencer have a warm and loving relationship that is built on friendship. They have known each other since childhood and their families are close. Although they have been together since their early twenties, they each had several relationships beforehand. They enjoy each other's company and engage in many joint activities, both as a couple and with their family and friends. When Carrie travels to Europe on business they miss each other but are not concerned about fidelity because of their mutual trust. They share plans and responsibilities, and support each other.

- Is security your highest goal?
- Would you find such a close relationship too boring?
- Do you need spice and romance in your relationships?

## Scenario 2: Spontaneous fun

Linda and Dan met at a mutual friend's party quite recently and started a relationship straightaway. They have both had a number of relationships and know that theirs is based on a desire to have fun. Dan, particularly, loves to act on impulse. They plan when to see each other but leave the decision about what to do to the last minute. Linda, who has recently left a long-term relationship that dissolved because both partners became bored, is reinvigorated by the relationship and the surprises that characterize it.

- Is spontaneity important to you?
- Do you think spontaneity is irresponsible?
- Do you like everything in life to be planned ?

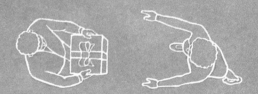

## Scenario 3: Successful partnership

Barbara and Ray met at work many years ago and decided to set up in business together as garden designers. They spend most of each working day together. When they get home, they both need time to themselves: Ray works in his studio while Barbara has her own sitting room. While they enjoy joint activities on the weekend, they make a point of following their separate interests during the weekday evenings.

- Are you happy being away from your partner?
- Are you concerned about your partner's faithfulness to you?
- Do you worry about losing any connection with your partner?

## Scenario 4: A passionate union

Diana and Robin started dating at college. Now in their mid-twenties, they have bought a house together. Their relationship has always been very passionate—they often have strong disagreements and end up in bed afterward. They have developed intimacy and trust but know that the main energy within their relationship is sexual. They have a lively social life, both together and separately. The demands of their careers mean that they have phases where one of them does all the chores.

- Is a lively sex life vital to you?
- Do you enjoy flexibility in your relationships?
- Do you dislike disagreeing with your partner?

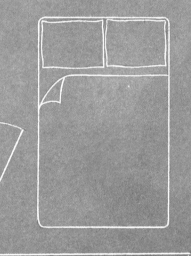

## Scenario 5: A happy balance

Millie and Toby used to live in next-door apartments and became involved when Millie needed help finding a carpenter. Toby offered to help Millie himself. Since then they have moved in together. Millie is attracted to Toby's abilities and confidence. Toby likes to feel useful to Millie, who is an impractical person. They have many friends, most of whom Toby knew before he met Millie. Toby makes most of the decisions in their relationship.

- Do you want to be needed by your partner?
- Do you want a partner to take care of you?
- Do you fear that your independence might be stripped from you in a relationship?

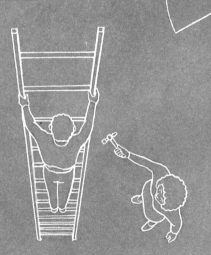

# RISKY RELATIONSHIPS

HERE IS ALWAYS RISK involved in loving someone. Will the relationship last? Do you dare become too involved? While no one can ever be sure of the answers to these questions at the outset, there are relationships that carry more obvious risks.

Relationships that are good for you provide two equal partners with a healthy degree of mutual dependency, combined with a certain amount of independence. Both partners are supportive; neither is "in control." There is flexibility, understanding, and a respect for each other's individuality.

Although these requirements seem simple, most of us have been involved in relationships that are not so well-balanced. These are the risky relationships.

However, although most people find themselves in one of the risky categories, many of these relationships are long-lasting, and can be happy. What matters is the degree of imbalance: the greater it is, the more likely it is to cause unhappiness and result in permanent breakdown. It helps, therefore, to identify which category your own relationship falls into, and to find ways to correct the imbalance while you are still loving and happy. Most risky relationships fall into one of six types, which are described below.

## The rescuing relationship

Some people want to be looked after, and some people like to care for others. A relationship between these two types can appear to be made in heaven. Indeed, many couples who answer this description feel that they have found their soul mates.

The risk lies within the imbalances of power and support. The caring partner is usually a benign mother or father figure, who makes most of the decisions. While this may suit them both for a while, unhappiness results when changes in either person make the balance uncomfortable. The rescued partner may feel irritated or unconsidered, or the caring partner can feel burdened by responsibility. Because care and support all go one way, it may be difficult for the parental person to show weakness and a need for nurture. As in all risky patterns, the need to take defined roles within the relationship inhibits development. If one of the two grows out of the role, the relationship falls apart.

*A flawed partnership*
*Certain types of relationships are unbalanced and unlikely to survive.*

*A heavy burden*
*It is unhealthy for one person in a relationship to be the one constantly giving support.*

If your relationship shows signs of this pattern, the sooner you are able to experiment with switching roles, the more likely you are to correct the imbalance and go on to develop a more healthy, balanced relationship.

## The dominating relationship

In this relationship, the need for control is even more apparent. One person is in charge—an obvious bully—and the other is expected to give in. Sometimes this starts out as a more kindly rescuing relationship, and then deteriorates.

It might be surprising that some people seem to choose such relationships over and over again, and are prepared to put up with what others find insupportable. As with most relationship patterns, this one can be traced back to childhood. Both people involved usually have problems with self-esteem. One gains a version of self-esteem by bullying, while the other feels he or she deserves no better. Despite the bully's apparent confidence, both partners are insecure and fearful of change, which is often what gives the relationship its durability.

*Total control*
*Some people have to live in the shadow of their overbearing partner.*

The only way for this relationship to change for the better is for the underdog to become more assertive. Sometimes this happens, but she or he then turns into a similar sort of bully. Learning that assertiveness includes a compassionate regard for the other person's feelings and needs is absolutely essential. Standing up to bullying tactics early enough in a relationship, and using the fear of parting to renegotiate a better way of handling the power balance may make a difference.

## The suffocating relationship

Some people believe that the most fulfilling kind of relationship is an exceptionally close one, in which both people think alike on every subject, never have a cross or impatient word, and need no other close friendships. But while harmonious views do matter, the fear of showing any differences can be stifling.

*Breaking free*
*If partners become too reliant on one another, the relationship can become oppressive.*

In common with other risky relationships, this one denies the individuality of each partner. Neither can change or develop without seeming threatening to the other. Both are likely to be nervous about conflict, either because they came from families who never argued, or because as children they were frightened by the reverse—parents who were always fighting.

It may be difficult to spot such a pattern at its inception because a characteristic of the first stages of love is just such an intense and exclusive closeness. If it continues after this phase has passed, however, then it is time to examine what is so worrying about allowing yourselves more leeway. It is healthy to cultivate some individual interests and see friends separately, as well as to explore personal likes and dislikes, seeing differences as a way of enriching the relationship, rather than diminishing it.

## The idealizing relationship

When you are first in love, your partner seems to embody perfection. In an idealizing relationship it is important for one of the partners to continue to place the other on a pedestal. This person remains adoring about even the most flawed partner.

This may be extremely satisfying to both people for some time. The difficulty is that the worshipper usually suffers from low self-esteem, believing that he or she is lucky to be with a perfect partner. Curiously, the idol is usually harboring a similar lack of confidence, and needs to be adored to cope with uncomfortable feelings.

The result is a lack of intimacy. The perfect one must retain the illusion by fitting in with the fantasy of the partner. The worshipper will often put up with unreasonable behavior because his or her confidence continues to ebb.

Recognizing that no one is perfect starts the process of change. The idol must be prepared to reveal feet of clay—and know that this is acceptable. The other partner needs to recognize and value what qualities she or he has that are estimable. A more realistic evaluation of themselves and each other leads to a more equal relationship.

***Perfection personified***
*Nobody can be expected to live up to a perfect image, and both people in a relationship must accept that they have faults.*

## The martyring relationship

There are people who enjoy doing things to make others happy. Somewhere along the line, for some of them, this becomes a less healthy desire to martyr themselves—administering to others even when it means being miserable.

When one person is a martyr in a relationship neither is happy. The martyr makes a virtue of this, while the other partner finds having his or her needs met so assiduously strangely uncomfortable. The martyr even seems to encourage bad behavior. This can be nipped in the bud early on if both

***Supporting role***
*The weight of responsibility within a relationship should fall on both partners equally.*

people understand what is happening. The martyr needs to recognize when doing something for a loved one has tipped over into becoming a chore. Recognizing that he or she also deserves love, attention, and cosseting—and learning to ask for them in an agreeable way—is the most helpful start. The other person needs to realize that an unselfish consideration for his or her partner will increase happiness for them both. Understanding that a relationship can't be happy unless both people concerned are happy is vital.

## The detached relationship

The opposite of an intensely close relationship is one in which both partners seem to need little from each other. Sometimes a relationship is like this from the start; it may also develop when problems

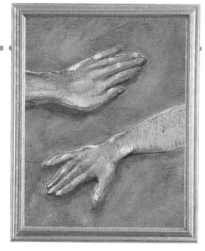

***Apart together***
*People often find that they are existing as totally detached entities within a relationship.*

cause the couple to cut off emotionally from each other. Some of these relationships are short-term, but in other cases the couple have been together for decades and raised a family, yet still do not develop a real intimacy.

People who are prepared to tolerate enduring relationships of this kind are often scared of needing too much from anyone else. Perhaps they felt unloved as children, or came from unstable and unsupportive families. While they are prepared to make a practical commitment, opening up to love is much harder.

Partnerships like this can and do last, but the people involved are denied the greater rewards of affection. If the couple are going to split up, they do so with less anguish than others. They might mourn the disruption of their lives, but their hearts are relatively unaffected.

## Sharing your thoughts

If your relationship appears to be going along any of these lines, and you don't want to miss out on the joys of loving interdependence, then you need to make efforts to become closer to your partner. Sharing your most private thoughts and asking for things that you need from your partner can often be difficult, particularly when you feel vulnerable, but the results are worth it. Doing more together, so that your lives entwine, will increase trust and happiness.

All relationships mature and change, as they must if they are going to survive. In the natural rhythm of things, possibilities are bound to open up for you to reassess your relationship and to work hard toward improving it. Even a relationship that has begun to feel unstable, therefore, can often be transformed by two people who are willing to make the effort.

# EARLY WARNING SIGNS

If you are not sure whether your relationship is in a high-risk category, consider these points.

- Do you feel unable to be yourself?
- Do you find it hard to make it clear that certain of your partner's thoughts or feelings are unacceptable to you?
- Does one of you invariably get your own way?
- Do you feel you do not get as much support as you give?
- Does either of you find it difficult to cope with your partner's interest in other friends or activities?
- Do you see one of you as the "strong" one and the other as "weak"?
- Do disagreements make you frightened or outraged?
- Do you feel that your relationship should never change in any aspect?
- Do you feel it is normal to be unhappy or bored in a long-term relationship?
- Would you rather put up with an unsatisfactory relationship than be without a partner?

If you answered "yes" to any of these questions, it suggests that there are risk factors in your relationship. Becoming aware of them allows you to make decisions about what you want to change to improve matters.

# THE TRUE LONELY-HEARTS AD

To get an idea of where your relationships are going wrong, compose two make-believe lonely-hearts advertisements: one for the kind of person that, in reality, you tend to become involved with, and another one for your ideal mate. Comparing the two can be very revealing.

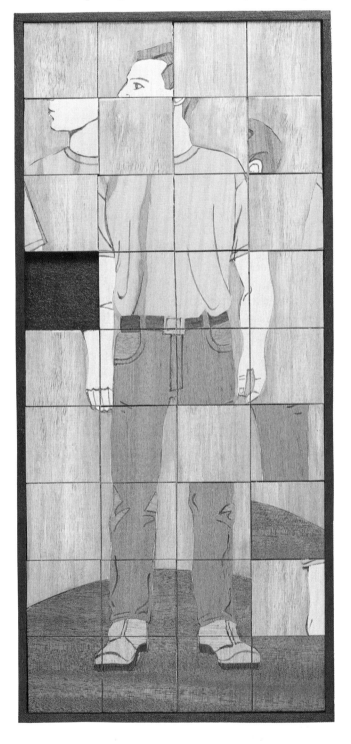

## Compiling a partner profile

Begin by thinking back over all your unsuccessful relationships to see whether any recognizable patterns emerge. Jot down the names of your past partners, then add your present one. Beside each name, list the characteristics that caused you particular unhappiness. Try to be as precise as possible: "swine," for example, is not clear enough. Think, instead, of more specific qualities such as "selfishness," "cruelty," or "coldness."

When you have finished, read back through your notes and mark any of these qualities that tend to reappear. Remember that some words, although different, essentially refer to the same trait: insensitivity and thoughtlessness, for instance, both describe a lack of care about other people's feelings. Now compile a list of these recurring traits; this will give you a profile of emotionally dangerous personality traits that you are consistently attracted to. You will see, for example, whether you tend to be drawn to people who are unfaithful, hypercritical, or self-absorbed.

At this point, it might be useful to consider how each of your partners in turn compares with this overall profile: Do some match up more closely than others? Were these the most painful relationships? Are your relationships becoming more or less successful as you get older?

## Pictures of the past

This is where the fun starts. Using the partner profile you have just created, prepare a lonely-hearts advertisement for this composite personality. For example: Selfish, arrogant, unreliable man required with a convincing line in meaningless flattery; must shirk responsibility and avoid blame at all costs. Make sure that you list only those characteristics that have come out of your partner profile. Enjoy this part of the exercise: it might shake a few skeletons out of their cupboards. It is also part of the

*Putting the pieces together*
*Working out which damaging emotional characteristics are common to all your relationships will help you to build up a personality profile of the unsuitable partners you tend to attract.*

## Worries wanted

*To get a clear picture of the kind of relationships you choose, set out the dominant characteristics of your previous partners in the form of a lonely-hearts advertisement.*

healing process because it helps you to identify which of your needs are not being met, and understand the signals you have been giving out about the kind of partner you are seeking. This is the first step toward changing your patterns from negative to positive.

When you have completed this profile, write another ad for the kind of person you really want, making it echo, wherever possible, the format of the one you did first. You can then compare the two to discover whether there is a sizeable gap between what you think you want and what you are actually seeking. Do you, for example, claim to want an independent and responsible woman when nearly all your partners have been vulnerable and clinging? Remember that you haven't ended up with your partners by accident—you have chosen them.

In retrospect, the very things that you now see as negative about your ex-partners are often the things that attracted you in the first place. For example, the clinging vine may have struck you initially as touchingly vulnerable and in need of your strength and support; similarly, "hooking" notoriously promiscuous men may boost your ego.

SELFISH, unreliable man with inability to care about anyone else, and tendency to leave clothes all over the floor, required by caring martyr with low self-esteem.

INSINCERE, thoughtless, egocentric woman incapable of being warm or supportive desired by vulnerable, sensitive man.

MARRIED man who expects someone at his sexual beck and call, and who promises to leave his wife but never will, urgently wanted by woman scared of intimacy and commitment.

SMOTHERING, over-possessive wife desperately needed by 35-year-old man who has never grown up and cannot take responsibility for his own life.

INARTICULATE moron with slobbish habits and bad temper wanted to provide constant arguments, tears, and unhappiness.

BRAINLESS, silly companion with devastating looks, great body, and inability to make intelligent conversation desired by man who can't cope with the competition of an equal partner and who needs an adoring admirer.

## Understanding the pay-off

If you consistently choose people who differ enormously from your ideal, you are probably getting some kind of pay-off from their apparently negative characteristics. In the early stages of a relationship, you may enjoy taking care of another person, rescuing her and sorting out her problems; or you could get a thrill from feeling you have tamed a seemingly incurable Casanova. Your pay-off, however, is short-lived, and you end up feeling unhappy and trapped by the very characteristics that gave you positive feelings in the beginning.

Another common mistake is to think that you can change the bits of your partner you don't like: Once you have solved her problems she will be strong and independent; once you have woven your spell, your Casanova will not require any other woman. But leopards do not change their spots, and, inevitably, you end up getting hurt. Learning to understand why you have chosen your partners, and what pay-off you receive from them, will free you to make new and better choices.

# SHADOWS FROM YOUR PAST

IN THE STUDY OF RELATIONSHIPS, psychotherapists and counselors place great emphasis on the impact of the past on the present, in the belief that early relationships have a lasting influence on our adult intimacies and even on the way we relate to our children. Marital therapists suggest that this particular type of family inheritance is like carrying a relationship framework in your mind that contains a complicated picture of how you see the connections between yourself and others. Each person's framework is uniquely his or her own, colored by his or her character as well as individual experience. And although you are constantly adding new parts to the picture as you meet new people and your existing relationships change, the foundations were set by your early experience.

It is argued that during these impressionable years children consciously and unconsciously absorb a great deal of what is going on around them—hardly surprising, given how small and vulnerable they are. For instance, rejection or acceptance from parents is literally a survival issue for a small child. In this narrow world of childhood, the relationship between your parents provides the first model of a partnership between a man and a woman. Your position in relation to your siblings or as an only child may still influence how you see yourself compared to others. Information about gender, sexuality, and intimacy are first broadcast and received in the home. The way your feelings were handled or dismissed, how punishment was meted out or praise was withheld also contributed to your self-image. These childhood experiences are but a few of the first pictures within the frame, and they will never be lost, although they may be masked by newer, updated images.

When two people get together, each brings an individual framework—that is, a set of ideas and expectations based on personal experience—to the relationship. When two people from a similar background and with similar interests get together the two pictures may well match.

## Illuminate your past
*Everything that has happened in your past, especially during your childhood, influences and colors your attitudes and reactions, particularly when it comes to forming relationships.*

But differences are often found under the surface. Generally, it is only when problems loom that a matching picture turns out to be only superficially so. This often shocks one or both partners, who suddenly find that the person they're attached to is rather different from the person that they thought they were.

## Restrictive frameworks

A definitive indicator to the chances of a relationship weathering inevitable storms is the extent to which each partner is able to reflect on his or her own part in any problems that arise. One major block to acknowledging this responsibility is that your view is so often clouded by your own vision of what a relationship should be, and how people should behave. Much of the time this view is heavily colored by handed-down notions, which—like hand-me-down clothes—might not fit their new owners at all. In other words, your chances of living happily together rely less on the amount of difference and similarity between you and more on your ability to recognize the benefits and limitations of previous patterns. In short, you must have the self-awareness and courage to step outside the frame.

One of the ways by which counselors gauge what you are likely to bring to new partnerships is to draw up a map of the generations or a "family profile." By asking questions about each partner's early life story and those of his or her parents and grandparents, and by looking for patterns of behavior that recur, it becomes easier to understand the emotional baggage that each person carries, and so to be more aware of potential problems that might arise.

On the following pages we show you how to draw up a family profile for yourself and your partner, and to help you to do so we give you several sets of questions to ask

yourself and each other. This is of course no insurance against the effects that life's upheavals will have on you both. But what the family profile may help you do is to think about your histories in detail, and to explore how these have contributed to your view of the world of relationships. You may also be able to see how past events have contributed to present problems and of course to present happinesses, and to locate preconceived ideas that have outlived their use and are ready to be discarded.

# Exploring Your Family Framework

By taking a detailed look at your childhood, and examining your attitudes to the relationships that you witnessed as a child, you and your partner can discover how many of your attitudes are unwitting re-enactments of old messages, rather than flexible approaches to new situations. This increased insight can provide you with greater understanding when conflict arises, enabling you to react in a more considered way.

## Drawing your family tree

In order to scrutinize your childhood influences you should start by roughly drawing your family tree on a large sheet of paper. Put in your immediate family: your partner, your children, your brothers and sisters. Mark in your own parents and their siblings. You don't need drawing skills for this—you might find it quickest to draw all the females as a circle, and all the males as a square.

Leave ample room around each one for notes. If you cannot remember various family connections, you can always simply write down a list of all the family members, generation by generation, who featured in your upbringing.

## Questioning your past

Once you have drawn your family tree, look at the "Examine Your Family Profile" questions on the right to help you to think in greater detail about your past. The questions are split into five sections. Some sections might be more useful than others, but the more willing you are to explore each one, the more helpful you will find this questionnaire. Remember, the starting point of the exercise is not what you feel now. You need to look at what you felt in the past, what pattern of relating was formed then, and what all-too-familiar emotions have always restricted your freedom of action.

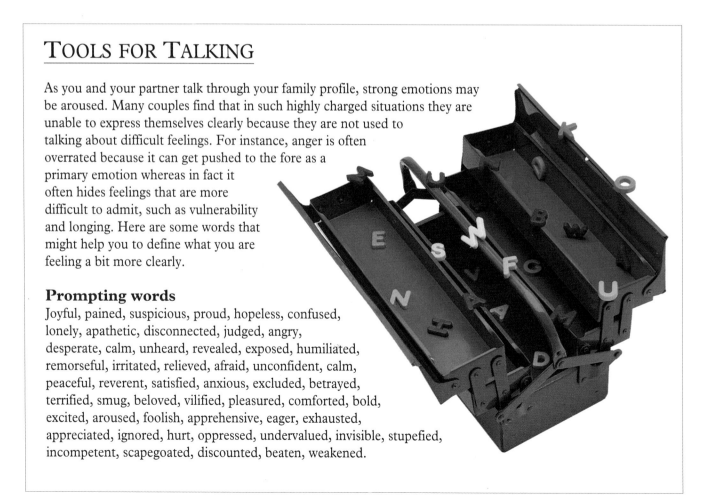

## Tools for Talking

As you and your partner talk through your family profile, strong emotions may be aroused. Many couples find that in such highly charged situations they are unable to express themselves clearly because they are not used to talking about difficult feelings. For instance, anger is often overrated because it can get pushed to the fore as a primary emotion whereas in fact it often hides feelings that are more difficult to admit, such as vulnerability and longing. Here are some words that might help you to define what you are feeling a bit more clearly.

### Prompting words

Joyful, pained, suspicious, proud, hopeless, confused, lonely, apathetic, disconnected, judged, angry, desperate, calm, unheard, revealed, exposed, humiliated, remorseful, irritated, relieved, afraid, unconfident, calm, peaceful, reverent, satisfied, anxious, excluded, betrayed, terrified, smug, beloved, vilified, pleasured, comforted, bold, excited, aroused, foolish, apprehensive, eager, exhausted, appreciated, ignored, hurt, oppressed, undervalued, invisible, stupefied, incompetent, scapegoated, discounted, beaten, weakened.

# EXAMINE YOUR FAMILY PROFILE

## Power and vulnerability

**1.** Whom would you pinpoint as the most powerful member of your family?
**2.** What was the power based on (e.g. wealth, age, education)?
**3.** Who seems powerful, but isn't really?
**4.** Who appears to be powerless while wielding considerable power?
**5.** How was power used?
**6.** How was power avoided or denied?
**7.** What was considered a "weakness" in your family?
**8.** Who was in competition with whom?
**9.** How was vulnerability dealt with? Was it respected or derided?
**10.** How were children punished, and what for?

## Men and women

**1.** What did you have to do to become an adult man or woman in your family (e.g. get married; stand up to your mother; you felt that you never could be considered one)?
**2.** Did men and women show their feelings differently?
**3.** What did the family believe men and women should do in the world?
**4.** What did the family believe men and women should do in relationships?
**5.** Did that change as people grew old?
**6.** What roles did the men and women play in relation to money?
**7.** What were the roles apportioned to men and women around sex (e.g. initiating it, hating it, being promiscuous)?
**8.** Were the educational or career expectations different for men and women?
**9.** Were the bosses male or female?
**10.** Could you come up with a few words that summarize how each sex treated the other (e.g. violently, distantly, tenderly)?

## Saints and sinners

**1.** Who were the family heroes/heroines?
**2.** For what were they honored?
**3.** Who were the family sinners?
**4.** What were their crimes?

**5.** How did the family ostracize its members?
**6.** Plot the family feuds and divisions.
**7.** Who were the rebels in the family?
**8.** What did you have to do to be included in the inner circle?
**9.** Who has shown the most self-sacrifice and loyalty?
**10.** Who has chosen to leave the family, and why?

## Roles in the family

**1.** What was your birth position in the family (oldest, middle, youngest)?
**2.** What did you see as your role (e.g. pacifier, clown, achiever)?
**3.** What did you have to do to be rewarded?
**4.** Which were stronger, the bonds between the adult partners or between the parents and children?
**5.** Were you closer to your same-sex or opposite-sex parent?
**6.** If you were an only child, what did you miss out on?
**7.** Among the children, who got the blame? Who got off?
**8.** How were roles divided between your parents (e.g. soft touch, unavailable, bad-tempered)?
**9.** Was anyone co-opted as a substitute parent?
**10.** Was there a make-up child for a lost baby?

## Life and death

**1.** Were there any problems relating to fertility and childbirth?
**2.** Were there any children who died (include miscarriages and stillbirths)?
**3.** Were there any suicides?
**4.** Were deaths talked about?
**5.** Where did depression or breakdowns locate themselves in the family?
**6.** Were there any trigger events?
**7.** Did anyone survive against the odds?
**8.** Was anyone seen to be to blame for anyone else's death?
**9.** Are there patterns of specific physical complaints throughout the family?
**10.** Is there anyone you wanted to die?

## Talking point

You may find it more fun to run through the family profile questions together, discussing the way you see your own or each other's families; or you may want to do your own answer sheets separately and compare notes. In answer to each of the questions, just write down one or two words that sum up the situation and your feelings about it; you can then use these as prompt notes, so you can talk about what you find. If you are going through a bad patch with your partner or a family member, call a ceasefire, and find a quiet time to look at your respective family profiles together.

You might have to complete several sections of the profile questions to begin to understand exactly what you are doing. Perhaps the section entitled "Power and vulnerability" reveals how difficult it is for you to admit your error, because as a child that was just what your parents insisted that you do. Or there might be a gender issue that needs an up-to-date solution: it could have been that men could do things in your family that women couldn't do, or

## CASE HISTORY: CONFLICT AND GROWTH

Peter and Maggie's marriage is pretty good but the way that each deals with anger promises to cause more of a rift between them than the issues they row about. Peter deals with anger by biting his lip and withdrawing into his study. Maggie is prone to dramatic temper tantrums. Peter and Maggie worked out separate family profiles and compared notes.

For Peter, the "Power and vulnerability" section of the profile exercise was very revealing. No-one was allowed open displays of emotion in Peter's family. If he ever lost his temper, as small boys do, his mother would go coldly quiet and send him to his room. Peter became almost tearful when he remembered how cut off and isolated he had felt. Peter realized how he had been re-playing the part of his own mother when he walked away from Maggie's anger. He agreed that he had been passing on an out-of-date scenario that now could play no useful part in an adult relationship. Peter was eventually honest enough to say, as Maggie had suspected, that there was an element of goading on his side before a row. By contrast, Maggie came from a large family in

which no one ever shut up. Emotions were certainly expressed openly, but finer feelings were often ridiculed in the process. As the only daughter of parents who seemed to favor the boys of the family, she had often felt ignored and overlooked. For Maggie, both the "Role in the family" and the "Men and women" questions revealed how every little disagreement with Peter evoked the message "You're a girl: you don't count," which typified her childhood experience. It was a long and slow process of sorting out the past from the present that lead to Maggie's finally realizing she was no longer an underdog. She discovered that she did not need to react in dramatic ways in order to be heard.

*Maternal influences*
*Maggie was raised in a lively household but she felt that her brothers were given most of the attention. She was expected to follow the same life-pattern as her housewife mother. Peter's mother suppressed any shows of emotion, considering them to be a sign of weakness.*

vice-versa. Or perhaps your family prescribed moral values that do not fit your present scenario, and are causing conflict. Explore these particular issues in the "Saints and sinners" section.

It could be that you haven't yet explored how your place in the birth order has left its mark on you, so you are forever the carer—or the outsider—which greatly affects your behavior now. The "Roles in the family" section is intended to reveal whether you are still carrying that particular burden as an adult. Although the "Life and death" section may appear overly serious, you'll be surprised how positive it can be to discover how happy events, such as a wedding or the birth of a child, can be marred by a sense of foreboding merely because the occasions tend to rattle skeletons in the cupboard.

Exploring your family profile will enable you to have a greater understanding of the attitudes that you bring to all of your relationships. This, in turn, will enable you to identify out-of-date, inappropriate attitudes that need changing.

## CASE HISTORY: MISTAKEN IDENTITY

Suzanne started seeing a counselor because she was having trouble making relationships that lasted. She was 35, and was thinking in terms of starting a family before it was too late. She reported no difficulty in finding men; they were initially charmed by her prettiness and affability. But none of them seemed to take her seriously. She appeared to be much in demand as a mistress, but never as a wife. Her latest boyfriend had broken off their relationship because of Suzanne's insistence on getting her own way, and her refusal to put other people first on occasion.

Suzanne drew up a family profile and showed it to her counselor. He was particularly struck by her position in her family of origin. She was the youngest of four children. The oldest two were boys, followed by a girl. Their mother then had three miscarriages before baby Suzanne was safely delivered. Mother's spirits were restored by the new arrival, who was petted and nursed to the exclusion of everyone, particularly the other daughter, who felt badly upstaged. The words she had jotted down about the other members of her family showed that Suzanne had grown up with a sense of her own specialness.

Slowly she realized how inappropriate this role model had become. Instead of behaving like a grown-up woman with a grown-up man, she treated every man like a soft-hearted older brother who would always give in to her. Expecting the disapprobation of women her own age, she found companionship with older, motherly women. Suzanne confessed to avoiding friendships with women in her peer group, therefore adding to her loneliness. She began to realize that in order to begin to make adult relationships, she had to abandon the old role model.

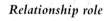

***Relationship role***
*Suzanne was pampered by her mother and brothers, while her father favored her sister Christine, who was often left out by her siblings. This relationship between her father and Christine could have set the pattern for Suzanne's adult role as "the other woman."*

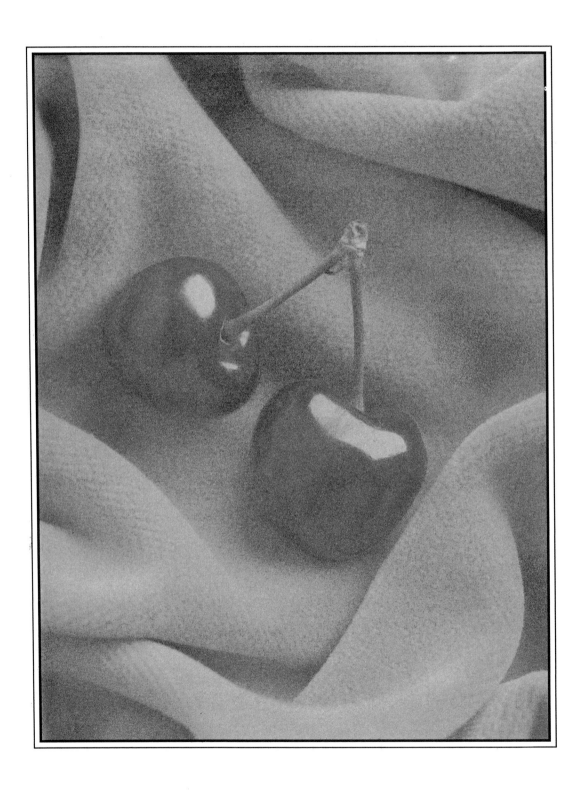

# CHAPTER THREE

# GETTING ON

THIS CHAPTER LOOKS at fully established relationships. It examines the ingredients that go into making up a strong and loving partnership, and the difficulties that beset all couples at some point. The two-part questionnaire "How Well Do You Know Each Other?" (pp. 74-77) allows you to examine both your own and your partner's views on such important issues as money, work, friends, and social life. The questionnaire reveals how well you know each other.

No matter how much two people love one another, it is unrealistic to expect a long-term union to be free of friction or disagreements. But discord needn't mean disaster: Working through problems and finding ways of accommodating both partners' needs will actually strengthen the foundations of a relationship. "The Art of Negotiation" (see pp. 100-103) helps you learn how to deal with misunderstandings and difficulties.

There is no doubt that good communication is the key to building a successful and harmonious relationship. The best way to resolve a problem is to talk about it with your partner. All too frequently, however, and despite the best intentions, the conversation becomes sidetracked into fault-finding and mutual recriminations. Even though you think you know each other well, often neither of you seems able to get your point across. How can two people who share many interests and opinions end up getting their wires badly crossed?

In fact, many couples do not actually say what they mean, even if they think they do. In addition, men and women often have such disparate conversational styles that they may interpret almost any comment quite differently. But communication is not an intractable problem: by completing the "What's Bugging You?" questionnaire (see pp. 82-85), you will be able to identify what level of dissatisfaction you are really expressing when you and your partner argue about apparently trivial issues.

Why do some relationships crumble at the first sign of trouble, while others seem to gain force from the readiness of both partners to deal with adversity? This chapter reveals that, while there is no single magic ingredient found in all good relationships, there are several crucial factors that contribute to success (see "The Vital Ingredients," pp. 96-99). "The Relationships Charter" on page 99 offers useful guidelines to help you achieve a rewarding and enduring partnership.

IN A GOOD RELATIONSHIP, THE BOND BETWEEN THE PARTNERS

PROVIDES SOLIDARITY AND MUTUAL SUPPORT

WITHOUT CRAMPING INDIVIDUAL DEVELOPMENT.

# DO YOU KNOW YOUR PARTNER?

I N ORDER TO FIND OUT HOW WELL you and your partner know each other, both of you should write down your answers to the questions below. After you finish, work through the questions again, this time trying to guess how the other person responded. How often did your partner answer in the way you expected? You might be pleasantly surprised to discover that your partner holds views similar to yours on issues that you thought you differed on and had avoided discussing out of fear of a confrontation. Conversely, some of his or her opinions may shock you. Use this starting point to discuss openly and honestly any issues that mean a great deal to you.

## WHO ARE YOU?

### Relationship

**1.** Do you feel hurt and disregarded if your partner doesn't ask you about your day?
**2.** Do you find it easy to accept your partner's opinions when they are different from your own?
**3.** Should a couple do everything together?
**4.** Do you believe that a couple should always be absolutely honest and open with each other?
**5.** Rate the importance you give to sex in your relationship on a scale from 0-10.
**6.** Rate the importance you give to talking in your relationship on a scale from 0-10.
**7.** Rate the importance you give to social interaction with friends on a scale from 0-10.
**8.** Could you forgive your partner if he or she confessed to having been unfaithful?
**9.** Do you agree with the expression "Love Conquers All?"

### Money

**1.** Do you think that the main purpose of money is to ensure security?
**2.** Do you think that society is too materialistic?
**3.** Do you agree that the only time money is a problem is when you have too little?
**4.** Do you feel that the time to spend money is when you are young enough to enjoy it?
**5.** Do you think people respect the ability to make money more than other types of achievement?
**6.** Do you think the rich have a moral duty to give a percentage of their wealth to charity?

**7.** If you won a large sum of money, would you:
**a)** take a dream holiday?
**b)** put a deposit on somewhere to live?
**c)** buy stocks and shares?
**d)** buy an original work of art?
**e)** put half in a savings account and have fun with the rest?
**f)** buy wildly extravagant presents for yourself and your loved ones?
**g)** take a year's leave to discover your real self?

**8.** Do you agree that money poisons the spirit?

**9.** Do you think that a lasting, fulfilling relationship is more important than money and possessions?

## General

**1.** Is a woman's place in the home when her children are small?

**2.** Of all cruelty, which is the hardest to tolerate: cruelty to animals, cruelty to children, or cruelty to old people?

**3.** Would you say your first impressions about people are almost always accurate?

**4.** Do you agree that protection of the environment is one of the most urgent issues of today?

**5.** Do you believe that man's aggressive instinct is part of his genetic makeup?

**6.** Have feminism and the sexual revolution made relationships between men and women more equal or just created new problems?

**7.** Would you say that power always corrupts?

**8.** Do you think abortion is evil?

**9.** Which of the following is closest to your secret fantasy: to be a world-famous musician; to be a sports ace; to create a happy and contented environment for your family; to win the lottery; to write a critically-acclaimed novel?

## WHO AM I?

This is a two-handed questionnaire to find out how your view of yourself compares with your partner's view of you. First answer the questions yourself, then ask your partner to assess your qualities and character traits from his or her point of view. Together you can look at your strengths and weaknesses and identify which areas you could improve, then do the same for your partner.

## You yourself

**1.** Are you an extrovert, introvert, or something in between?

**2.** Would you describe yourself as an optimist?

**3.** Do you need to feel in control?

**4.** Are you a perfectionist?

**5.** Would you describe yourself as an adventurous, free spirit?

**6.** Are you a worrier?

**7.** Would you say you were basically secure?

**8.** Are you sensitive to other people's feelings?

**9.** Would you say you are kind?

**10.** Are you stubborn?

**11.** Do you have a bad temper?

**12.** Are you secretive?

**13.** Have you an envious nature?

**14.** Are you fundamentally lazy?

**15.** Would you call yourself neurotic?

**16.** Do you consider it essential to have a regular and predictable routine to your life?

17. Are you a loner?
18. Do you have an enquiring mind?
19. Do you have a fearful attitude to life?
20. Do small frustrations make you explode?
21. Are you easily discouraged?
22. Are you impatient?
23. Are you spontaneous?

## One-to-one

1. Is it easy for you to express your emotions?
2. Are you very jealous?
3. Do you seek constant reassurances of love and approval from those around you?
4. Do you bear grudges?

5. Are your moods often irrational?
6. Do you play power games?
7. Are you open about your needs and desires?
8. Do you use emotional blackmail?
9. Are you sensitive to your partner's feelings and emotional needs?
10. Do you harbor resentment?
11. Do you find it hard to admit you are wrong?
12. Do you vent bad moods and frustration on your partner?
13. Do you believe that your happiness is your partner's responsibility?
14. Does it upset you or make you angry if your partner wants to see his or her old friends alone?

**15.** Do you find yourself reading hidden motives and meanings into what your partner says?

**16.** Are you sexually manipulative? Do you use lovemaking to get what you want?

**17.** Do you find it hard to trust?

**18.** Do you think that true love means being understood without having to explain yourself?

**19.** Do explosive rows stir your passion?

**20.** Do you generally defer to your partner's opinions?

**21.** Do you think your partner understands most things about you?

**22.** Do you sulk?

**23.** Would you describe yourself as a good listener?

## At work

**1.** Do you panic in a crisis?

**2.** Would you say that you have a dedicated attitude to your job?

**3.** Are you highly ambitious?

**4.** Do you find it hard to delegate?

**5.** Do you work well in a team?

**6.** Do you feel that your work is the most important thing in your life?

**7.** Are you always punctual?

**8.** Which aspect is more important to you: job satisfaction or a high salary?

**9.** Are you easy to work with?

**10.** Do you find it easier to get on with colleagues of the opposite sex?

**11.** Are you a very different person in the workplace from the way you are at home?

**12.** Do you agree that corporate loyalty is essential in your working life?

**13.** Do you aspire to be a high-flier?

**14.** Does work generally take priority over the other areas of your life?

**15.** Do you feel that work is a treadmill?

**16.** Are you competitive?

**17.** Do you think that ruthlessness is a positive quality in the world of business?

**18.** Are you assertive and direct?

**19.** Would you describe your working style as:
  **a)** slow and deliberate?
  **b)** enthusiastic but rushed?
  **c)** somewhere in between?

**20.** Do you thrive on challenges?

**21.** Would you play hookey to go off for a picnic?

**22.** Do you feel you are working below your full potential in your current job?

**23.** Rate the satisfaction value of your work on a scale of 0–10.

## Socially

**1.** Are you gregarious?

**2.** Do you place a high value on friendship?

**3.** Do you prefer large social gatherings or seeing a few friends on their own?

**4.** Do you let your hair down at parties?

**5.** Do you enjoy your own company?

**6.** Does it throw you if people drop in on you unannounced?

**7.** Do you have a close friend of the opposite sex?

**8.** Do you enjoy a good gossip?

**9.** Do you find it easy to strike up conversation with a stranger?

**10.** Do you love being the center of attention?

**11.** Do you see entertaining as a way of displaying status and style?

**12.** Do you find conversation difficult with people of different views or from a different background than your own?

**13.** Do you tend to avoid direct eye contact?

**14.** Do you need a few drinks before you can relax in a social situation?

**15.** Do you like:
  **a)** all of your partner's friends?
  **b)** some of your partner's friends?
  **c)** none of your partner's friends?

**16.** Do you find that you often enjoy the planning and organizing of a dinner party or other social event more than the event itself?

**17.** Are you a flirt?

**18.** Do you prefer sticking with old friends to meeting new people?

**19.** Do you let yourself go when dancing?

**20.** Do you find that you worry about the impression you make on people?

**21.** Do you think that politeness and consideration to others are important?

**22.** Do you like wearing outrageous clothes when you go to a party?

**23.** Do you usually either love people or hate them—with nothing in between?

# ARE YOU COMMUNICATING?

A FEW YEARS BACK, a graffiti artist spray-painted "Make Love Not War" on a wall. Underneath, someone added the line: "I'm married. I do both." Anyone with experience of a one-to-one relationship will read this with a wry smile. They will also know that, for most couples, war means verbal conflict. And discord often erupts when a seemingly straightforward conversation suddenly springs ill-tempered verbal barbs.

Human beings show who they are, what they want, and why they behave as they do by language, facial expression, and gesture. At the "in love" stage of a relationship, when romance and sexual attraction are at a high, communication is probably as delightful and trouble free as everything else going on between you. As the relationship becomes established, however, misunderstandings inevitably start to manifest themselves. And things get worse as each unresolved misunderstanding prepares the ground for the next.

Most of the time, our conversations are spontaneous. We know what we want to say but we don't stop to work out how we are going to say it. For example, Jane tells Nick that a mutual friend has invited them to stay at her weekend cottage. "That's fine," Nick replies, but his intonation is flat and he is staring out of the window. Jane, who often worries that Nick finds their life together boring, interprets his manner of responding as con-

firmation of that fear. It also ignites her anger that he doesn't put more effort into their social life. For his part, Nick believes he has given a perfectly adequate response. His answer "That's fine," means just that. He said it in a flat tone because he was thinking about his tax return and not because he wanted to convey an indirect message. The conversation escalated into a row that had nothing to do with its original content.

## Hearing criticism

Similarly, it can often happen that criticism is heard when it isn't intended. A neighbor asked Jack to help him repair the porch roof. When he came back a couple of hours later, Caroline greeted him with the sighing remark that he always put himself at other people's beck and call. Jack has a pressured work life and Caroline's concern was that he didn't get enough rest and would make himself ill. Jack, however, interpreted her comment as meaning he

couldn't say no and was useless at handling people. His defensive reaction sparked a hostile exchange that would never have happened if she had expressed her anxiety about his health directly.

Caroline also misinterprets Jack's motives for interfering when she is cooking—something she can't stand. If she is chopping vegetables, he tells her she is holding the knife incorrectly; he objects to the way she seems to be doing three things at once; and he checks to see that she has remembered to turn off the gas. Jack's worry is that Caroline isn't careful enough and will have an accident. As far as Jack is concerned, he is simply pointing out the safest procedure for doing things. To Caroline, his "pointing out" implies that she is careless and inept.

### Communication gap
*It is all too easy to misinterpret each other's intentions, making it impossible to meet in the middle successfully. Communicating clearly and straightforwardly allows you to reach greater understanding.*

## Mixed memories

*For one person, dark rooms and traditional furnishings are delightful, evoking childhood memories of cozy winter evenings. But her partner loathes this atmosphere because it stirs up memories of a rigid and repressive upbringing.*

There are also occasions when criticism directed at an outside source is taken as a personal attack. When Jonathon managed to get tickets to take Naomi to a hot new play he was delighted. Discussing the performance afterward, however, Naomi said it hadn't lived up to her expectations and that she thought the lead actor was miscast. At the time, they had been living together for eight months and the first differences of opinion and taste were starting to surface. Alert to this, Jonathon took her criticism of the play not as an opening for interesting debate, but as criticism of himself and his attitudes. He felt that she was criticizing his artistic judgment and sensitivity to the play and the various performances. As a result he began defending the performance in an overly aggressive way, thus causing Naomi to take an increasingly adamant stance.

Praise can also be interpreted as indirect criticism. If your partner makes a complimentary remark about a member of the opposite sex, for example, you might feel this implies that you are somehow inferior in comparison. It can also happen when praise is given inappropriately. When Jenny's poems were rejected by a magazine, she was very dejected and Paul tried to cheer her up by reminding her what a talented illustrator she was. In this context, Jenny interpreted his words as telling her to forget what she couldn't do and concentrate on what she could. Her response was to rush off in tears, leaving Paul totally bewildered about what he had done to upset her.

## Causes of misunderstanding

Perfect understanding is a Utopian myth. We are all complicated individuals and everything we think is linked to all that has happened in our life. This is why two people can share an identical experience and yet form totally different views of it. Misunderstandings between couples generally have three main causes:

**1.** Each is putting his or her own interpretation on what the other thinks, feels, or intends.

**2.** Partners are not expressing themselves clearly or they are not saying what they mean.

**3.** Neither is listening to what the other says.

All too often we presume to know exactly what our partner is feeling. Instead of listening to what the other person is saying we make assumptions that have little to do with any actual words spoken. We "hear" only those things that prove our theory of what is going on in his or her head.

## I thought you agreed with me

*Robin had always assumed Irene liked sleeping entwined because that was what he liked. However she ended up feeling suffocated by being held so close and resorted to starting bedtime squabbles to keep him away.*

*That wasn't what I meant*

*A common form of not saying what you mean is telling your partner you don't mind about something when you do. When Jeremy asked Pat if she minded if he went for a day's fishing, she said no. In fact she resented it deeply. She felt her intonation expressed her real wish and she wanted Jeremy to pick up on that—but he didn't.*

## Learning to listen

Selective listening is something that, to a greater or lesser degree, we all do. We focus on what pleases or interests us, or on what confirms our feelings and convictions. In other words, we "hear what we want to hear." To be a good listener, however, you must give your full attention to whoever is talking. This means not switching off—for many, an automatic reflex when a partner nags, shouts, or becomes over-emotional—and not listening with half your mind somewhere else.

It is equally important to check that you really understand what is being said. This can be done by repeating what you think you've heard, giving your partner the opportunity to tell you whether your interpretation is correct. And if you haven't

understood, ask him or her to rephrase the remark or clarify it with an example.

Finally, it is important to think before offering comments and points of view. Opinions on matters of fact can be relevant, but opinions on someone else's feelings and motives are best left unexpressed. To accuse someone of being immature, spineless, neurotic, repressed, and so on, is wounding and unconstructive. Part of being a good listener is to respect the other's right to his or her feelings whether you approve of them or not.

## All-round communication skills

It is vital to be able to recognize when offence is intended and when it is not; otherwise you may overreact to a remark that is careless but not malicious. If you are honest with yourself and direct with your partner, you will know when you are instigating or being goaded into a confrontation, and when you are trying to hurt. Remember that provoking the other person is almost bound to lead to a row, and—as the row will probably not focus on the issue that really concerns you—you will still feel frustrated afterward.

Being able to listen generously, attentively, and uncritically is a valuable life skill. So is expressing yourself clearly and saying what you mean. Once you have mastered these skills, you will be equipped to deal with the misunderstandings and flare-ups that are a natural and inevitable part of any relationship.

*Listen to what I'm saying*

*One way of not saying what you mean is to make an issue out of something other than what is really bothering you. When Janice goes on about the amount of time Luke spends watching television, she is really complaining that she feels that he doesn't pay her nearly enough attention. Unfortunately, Luke isn't listening to her either way.*

# WHAT'S BUGGING YOU?

Some arguments that you have with your partner are hard to explain. "It sounds silly…," you say, as you report that finding your partner had finished the milk had started a row that lasted into the night, leaving you both feeling murderous. Perhaps you can't believe that you could get so worked up about something so apparently unimportant. But people really do claim that their marriage broke up because the top was always left off the toothpaste. A man really did kill his wife when she moved the mustard from its usual place. Are we actually so petty, or is there more to such rows than there seems?

### Erupting emotions
*Suppressed worries and resentments can flare up and explode, disguised as rows about trivial issues and domestic matters, such as who does the cleaning and why you didn't phone when you were late.*

The small matters of daily life certainly have significance. Minor irritations, constantly repeated, can be more aggravating than major bust-ups that happen only occasionally. When you are out of synch on issues that really affect your mood, it colors your perception of the relationship. But when these little things unleash great rage, and explosions of pain and anguish, then they are likely to be symptoms—outward signals that expose some graver, unresolved issue between you. Even if you are conscious that an argument seems out of all proportion to the apparent cause, you might be unaware of the deeper problem. The fact that your partner finished off the milk triggered an anxiety you had been feeling for some time: His selfishness means he doesn't really care about you; perhaps he doesn't love you anymore. You daren't dwell on this because it calls into question your entire relationship, and if you bring it out into the open you will have to face whether the relationship will come to an end.

On the other hand, you might know where your real anger lies, but don't want to provoke your partner by mentioning it. Or, if your self-esteem is low, you may not believe that you have the right to challenge your partner's behavior; somehow it seems easier to blow your top about the milk instead.

But arguing over trivialities only intensifies angry feelings about the deeper, underlying problem, which remains unresolved. Dealing with the real issue, on the other hand, is more likely to have a positive effect than the negative one you fear.

## What are you arguing about?

The following questionnaire helps you identify whether small squabbles are genuinely trivial and of little consequence, or whether they are indicative of something more important and fundamental. It also helps to pinpoint underlying issues about which each of you feels very differently. See which responses most closely match your own, then turn to page 138 to see what they mean.

**1. You argue constantly over who does what in the house. One of you claims to do the most; the other says it is shared fairly, or that standards are too high.**

*If you think you do the most, are you angry because:*
**a)** you want more time to do other things?
**b)** you believe your partner thinks it's your job?
**c)** you feel as if your partner doesn't consider your time to be important?

*If you think you do enough, are you angry because:*
**a)** you don't believe that all the tasks are necessary?
**b)** you think your partner is trying to control you?
**c)** you feel unappreciated?

**2. Rows arise because one of you thinks the other is late too often, or doesn't phone.**
*If your partner is late, are you angry because:*
**a)** you worry about your partner's safety?
**b)** you believe it shows a lack of concern for you?
**c)** you believe your partner's lateness indicates more interest in other people than in you?

*If you are angry because your partner complains about your lateness, is it because:*
**a)** it doesn't happen often, and is accidental?
**b)** you don't believe your partner understands your reasons for arriving late?
**c)** you believe your partner is trying to monitor you too closely?

**3. You argue because you have different ideas about how you should spend money, and one of you thinks the other is being irresponsible financially.**

*If you think your partner spends too much, are you angry because:*
**a)** money is short, and you can't pay the bills.
**b)** you think you should be consulted about expenditure, and money should be shared?
**c)** you believe your partner doesn't value what is important to you?

*If your partner says you spend too much, do you feel angry because:*
**a)** you think there is enough for essentials so it doesn't matter?
**b)** you sense that your independence would be curtailed along with your spending?
**c)** you think your partner is obsessed with money?

**4. Sex is a battleground. One of you wants more than the other, or at times when the other isn't interested.**

*If you are withholding sex, are you angry because:*
**a)** the sex you do have doesn't suit you any more?
**b)** you think your feelings aren't being considered?
**c)** you feel your partner just wants sex and it has nothing to do with love for you?

*If you are the one being denied sex, are you angry because:*
**a)** you need regular sex to feel relaxed and healthy?
**b)** if your partner doesn't want to make love, you think there must be someone else?
**c)** you feel unloved and unwanted when you are sexually rejected?

**5. You and your partner often clash over dates: one of you makes appointments without consulting the other, either for joint events or for solo engagements.**

*If you are angry about your partner's arrangements, is it because:*
**a)** you need to be consulted so that you can plan your time?
**b)** you believe your partner thinks your own plans are less important?
**c)** you believe your partner doesn't care whether you are put out or not?

*If you are angry because your partner complains about your arrangements, is it because:*
**a)** you didn't realize it was a problem?
**b)** you don't think you should have to ask your partner's permission as if you were a child before you make arrangements?
**c)** you feel as if your partner is attempting to curtail your freedom?

**6. One of you has a friend the other one doesn't like, and this causes friction.**

*If you disapprove of one of your partner's friends, is it because:*

**a)** it's a person you don't want to see?

**b)** you resent your partner's liking someone you don't like?

**c)** you believe your partner's feelings for the friend suggest you are of less value to your partner?

*If it is one of your friends who is disapproved of, are you angry because:*

**a)** it's a person you like and want to see?

**b)** you resent having your friendships controlled by someone else?

**c)** an attack on your friend makes you feel your partner doesn't care about what is important to you?

**7. There's often a battle over who watches what on the television. One of you objects to a program that the other wants to see.**

*If you are the one who objects to your partner's choice, is it because:*

**a)** there's something else you want to see?

**b)** you believe you always have to give in to your partner's wishes?

**c)** you believe your partner prefers watching television to talking to you?

*If your partner is objecting to what you want to watch, are you angry because:*

**a)** it's your favorite program?

**b)** you believe your partner is deliberately spoiling your enjoyment?

**c)** you believe your partner wants the television off so the two of you are able to discuss an issue that you find painful or difficult?

*Cooling heated tempers*
*Left unresolved, even apparently minor problems can lead to deep conflict. But good communication coupled with a willingness to build greater harmony will defuse destructive tension and suppressed anger, and improve mutual understanding.*

# ARE YOU BEING HEARD?

Successful, harmonious relationships form when people understand each other. Friction between partners who live together is normal, but when arguments blow up out of all proportion to an apparently insignificant cause, it is usually because one or both is being misunderstood.

Counselors often hear the words, "He (or she) knows I like (or need)..." whatever it might be, followed by the complaint that despite "knowing," the partner does nothing about it. It often emerges, however, that the issue has never been discussed directly. Typical ways people believe that they are making their feelings known is by behaving moodily, hinting, or picking a fight over a related but minor issue.

If you have roundabout ways of showing your feelings and needs, they might well be misinterpreted by your partner. This is a recipe for unresolved anger, which can only grow. Whenever you feel misunderstood by your partner, who seems to

---

**What they say**
**Mark:** "I bumped into Ted on the way home. He said he and some friends were eating out tonight and we were welcome to join them as well. Do you want to go?"
**June:** "Is it expensive?"
**Mark:** "No, there's a really cheap set-price menu."

---

**What they say**
**June:** "I've got some work I really ought to finish off this evening. You go on your own if you want to."
**Mark:** "OK! See you later."
*Mark leaves.*

---

---

**What they mean**
June is worried about money. She doesn't want to nag, but asking Mark whether the meal would be expensive is code for "We can't afford it." If Mark had asked the question, she feels she would have recognized the hint, and said "It's cheap, but I guess it's more than we can afford."

---

**What they mean**
If the positions were reversed, June feels she wouldn't go out. Mark misses the cue, and takes what June says at face value. June, not understanding that Mark has not received her message, feels hurt that she has to bear the burden of their finances, while Mark goes off and enjoys himself.

---

be blatantly flouting your wishes or ignoring your needs, you should ask yourself, "Am I making myself clear?" and "Am I being heard?" Once you recognize this as your problem, you will have taken the first step on the way to tackling it. If not, matters can get worse, as Mark and June found (see story outline, below). Like many couples, they sometimes assume that their true feelings and anxieties are obvious—even when they don't express them explicitly.

## The origins of argument

Instead of being clear about her worries, June assumes that Mark is aware of them, but is choosing to disregard them and please himself. Even if Mark did sense tension in June's manner, it would be likely to increase his desire to go out rather than say, "Is everything all right or is there a problem?" By the time Mark returns from his evening out, June is feeling resentful and ready to find fault with him. This intensifies when it becomes obvious that

### What they say

*When Mark returns, June is in bed, reading. Having had an enjoyable evening, Mark is in a good mood, and snuggles up to her.*
**June:** "How much have you had to drink?"
**Mark:** "Not much."
*He takes her book away and starts to kiss her.*

### What they say

**June:** *(explodes)* "I was reading that. You're so selfish all the time, you only ever think about what you want!"
**Mark:** "You're no fun anymore. All you think about is work!"
*They start to have a row.*

### What they mean

Asking Mark how much he had to drink is June's coded way of saying "How much did you spend?" June feels that Mark is blithely ignoring her concern, and, to add insult to injury, he makes it clear he wants sex.

### What they mean

June feels used and neglected and she really thinks Mark is being selfish. Mark, completely unaware of her feelings, is merely in a loving mood. He is oblivious to her misery and assumes she is becoming a killjoy.

he has had a good time, while she has spent a miserable evening alone. When Mark starts being affectionate toward her, June feels that he is interested only in his own needs and desires. When they start to row June brings up, among other things, the fact that he had gone out that evening. Mark claims she is being irrational and inconsistent—after all, she'd told him to go!

If this kind of scenario and argument is repeated often, the situation can deteriorate. Instead of telling Mark what is the matter directly, so that he could share in the responsibility for their finances, June became a "stern mother" showing by example how she wanted him to behave, and becoming even more upset and moody when he didn't follow her lead. Mark's reaction to her "irrationality" and withdrawal might lead him to behave in more ways that make her feel unloved and undervalued, and perhaps become more of the "irresponsible child" who lets her do all the worrying.

---

### What they could say
It would be much better if June tried to express her worries directly:

**June:** "We haven't got much money and I'm very worried about it."

**Mark:** "You're right. Let's talk about it."

---

### What they could say
**June:** "When you enjoy yourself without me, I get scared that you don't love me."

**Mark:** "I really needed a night out, but it would have been better if you'd been there. I love you and I always love being with you."

---

---

### What they mean
June's statement shows Mark the basic problem that she is really worried about and, because she doesn't start off by blaming him, it gives him a chance to respond positively without going on the defensive.

---

### What they mean
June is being honest about how vulnerable she feels when confronted by certain aspects of Mark's behavior. This shows him that she needs reassurance about his love for her, and not that she is a spoilsport who just doesn't want him to have fun.

## Avoiding assumptions

It is hard to avoid the assumption that, because your partner knows you well, he also knows what you are thinking and feeling. But when you consider it, can you always identify what you really want, or what lies beneath your anger? These feelings are unique to you: why you want what you want, and what makes you angry, frightened, or sad has to do with your personality, and all the experiences you have had in your life. It is a common mistake to believe that others "make" you angry, upset, or nervous. But they can only activate vulnerabilities that are already there. If Mark and June continue to get on one another's nerves, June might change from hinting at the problem to attacking him earlier: "You make me sick! You're so irresponsible. You don't care what I want as long as you're happy!"

## Learning to be direct

This kind of approach seems to be direct, but it isn't. If June had tried to explain that she was worried about their finances and felt hurt when he went out without her, she would have given Mark better insight into why she felt angry and frustrated with him. These statements would have been both honest and direct because they were about herself and her own reactions to what was happening. She would not have been blaming Mark, but illuminating what it was like to be her.

When there are good intentions and good feelings in a relationship, emotional directness allows a couple to get to the heart of issues, and to deal with them in a positive way. Sometimes this means a compromise. If June had told Mark that she was worried about money, he might have said, "I've had a terrible day at work and I really need some fun tonight." Then they could have evaluated the options. Perhaps they could do something fun together that wouldn't cost anything. Or June might have decided that Mark's feeling low was a good reason to spend a bit more than she would normally consider appropriate.

It can sometimes be difficult to stop a silly argument from spiralling out of control when you are in the middle of it. If you have had a difficult day and are not in a good mood, you are hardly likely to have the patience or inclination to look more

**Be prepared**
*You may both find it easier to talk calmly and present your views clearly if you agree on a time and date in advance when you will talk through any problems.*

deeply into the real problem. But if those tetchy exchanges are becoming more common, and affecting your feelings about the relationship, it helps to reflect on them once the moment has passed and you are feeling cooler. Look back on these rows and analyze what you were feeling, what you wanted, and how you expressed yourself. Resist the impulse to analyze too deeply what your partner said or meant, because you may well arrive at the wrong conclusion. Instead, try to figure out your own deeper motivations and what you actually said. Many angry feelings originate in hurt or fear, and these can be hard to talk about and easier to mask with rage or spite.

## Making a time to talk

Once you can identify where you might have gone wrong, and what you neglected to say, it helps to suggest a time to talk things over with your partner. Again, don't make the suggestion in the middle of an argument. Wait until you are having a pleasant time together and say something like, "I've been thinking about the crazy row we had the other night and I think perhaps I gave you the wrong impression about what was the matter. Can we talk about it?" It might suit you both to talk about it there and then, but if not say, "Let's fix a time, because I'd really like to clear things up."

Having time to prepare allows you to pick your words carefully. Talking solely about your own reactions and feelings, without sounding as though you blame your partner for them, is likely to create a climate in which your partner, too, can explain his or her feelings and motivations. Sharing how you feel in a generous spirit, helps your partner to understand you and "hear" you, while listening with equal generosity and care to what your partner has to say should make misunderstandings a thing of the past.

# DEALING WITH INFIDELITY

INFIDELITY HAS ALWAYS BEEN a fact of life: Surveys show that a third of men and a quarter of women admit to being unfaithful. Yet contained within these statistics are different types of infidelity—ranging from the one-off drunken fling to the serious affair that vies in commitment and importance with the marriage.

Degrees of seriousness vary, too. The opportunistic one-night stand away from home, which may mean little or nothing, is at the bottom of the scale. More important is the fling born out of sexual curiosity, or a brief affair, or series of them, to alleviate sexual boredom at home. Top of the scale is the more intense and long-lasting affair in which there is emotional as well as sexual infidelity.

### One life, two loves

*Having an affair may relieve sexual boredom but it is bound to cause emotional strain by pulling you in two directions and undermine the bond between you and your partner.*

## Why affairs happen

There are several categories of motivation that lead to an affair. The typical one-night stand, never to be repeated and happening in extraordinary circumstances might be exempt from categorization, although there could be deeply buried motivations at the heart of it. Perhaps the most obvious are the sex-based motives: You want to have sex with someone different, even though your sex life is good; or your sex life is disappointing and you look for excitement elsewhere. Some apparently sex-based motives are really emotional: although the encounter is purely sexual, you are actually looking for affirmation that you are still attractive or that you are not old.

In other cases the motivation is more obviously emotional, even when the affair has a high sexual content. You are not getting on with your partner and feel unappreciated: a lover restores your sense of self-worth. There can also be a desire for revenge: you are angry at your partner, and infidelity, even when secret, is a way of "paying back,"

making you feel one up on him or her. In certain cases, a fear of commitment and intimacy can make a monogamous relationship feel too close and threatening, so constantly having an affair on the go, even if the lovers change, can ensure you maintain the emotional distance you want in your primary relationship.

Finally, you might embark on an affair because you feel that your principal relationship is really over, yet you need to set up an alternative before you can face leaving. In this case, the affair may merely be a bridge to help you out of your main relationship. Once this has dissolved, the affair itself may end soon afterward.

Many affairs remain undiscovered. Even so, most have an impact on a relationship. A one-night stand or brief fling caused by sexual curiosity might not make ripples if your attitude is genuinely casual, but if it makes you feel guilty or devalued then your behavior will reflect this. Taking a lover to relieve sexual boredom has more long-term consequences: the boredom may lessen, but the problem in your relationship remains and even worsens, because you put no effort into improving it.

An affair that stems from a need to reaffirm your sense of your own attractiveness, youth, or self-worth could go either way. Increased self-esteem may lead you back to your relationship with a fresh determination to improve it and remain faithful. More likely, however, is that the very fact of receiving the support and confirmation you need elsewhere will serve to make you even more dissatisfied with your current partner. An affair that gives you what you need emotionally or intellectually can make your relationship seem more supportable but, as with sexual boredom, it means you rarely tackle the problems, which may worsen. When the affair ends, the deficiencies in the relationship may become unbearable.

## Out in the open

Secrecy in itself is damaging. Having to watch what you say, or telling lies, weakens the bond with your partner. The fact that you can be open with your lover, who knows the score, may make the affair seem even more intimate and necessary.

When infidelity is revealed, whether you have come clean or are discovered, a crisis always results. If you started the affair to make it easier for you to leave the relationship, this is usually when the break will come. But sometimes the last thing you wanted was to finish with your partner. Whether the affair was important to you or not, your partner is bound to feel betrayed, humiliated, frightened, and angry. You seem like a stranger and your relationship is called into question. A brief sexual adventure might be forgiven and forgotten—although there seems to be a gender difference here: on the whole, men seem less able to handle sexual betrayal, and are more likely to want to split up because of it. The more important the relationship is to you, either sexually or emotionally, the graver the crisis and the aftermath.

Whether to confess or not is no simple matter. If both of you rate honesty very highly then it may be the best option. Rebuilding your relationship then depends on whether the affair is over, whether the unfaithful partner is truly committed to making the relationship work, and whether the other partner feels there is enough love left between you to make the work worthwhile.

### Mark of betrayal
*Even the suspicion that your partner is having an affair can make you feel that you have lost the person you used to know and love.*

Confessing might not always be motivated by honesty however. If you tell to inflict hurt, to show off, or to share the burden of your guilt, it will do more harm than good. Confessing your infidelity as a way of making yourself feel better when you have no real intention of mending your ways simply creates hurt and confusion.

## Facing the facts

Once a partner knows about the affair there is always a question mark over whether the relationship will survive. If you still love each other, value the life you have built together, and believe there is hope for the future, the outcome looks good. In the midst of the crisis, you might not be sure whether any of these are true for you, yet you may be prepared to see if you can weather the storm. Whatever the case, your relationship is going to be different in the future. Counselors look on the discovery of an affair as similar to bereavement: what has died is the old relationship, and even when it emerges in better shape than before, the experience is like starting afresh together.

Some couples try to put the affair behind them and ignore it. In the long term, this is not very satisfactory. Buried grievances fester and unanswered questions continue to rankle. A relationship patched up in this way may last forever, but it rarely does so happily.

Counselors have found that facing the facts of an affair, however painful, is more likely to result in laying it to rest in a healthy way. Usually this means talking through the issues in the interest of understanding them, rather than trying to hurt or blame each other. It helps if the unfaithful partner is able to identify the motivation behind the infidelity, so that the basic problem can be identified. Both partners need to recognize that if something has been going wrong between them, then the responsibility is joint; the one who strayed is not necessarily more at fault than the one who didn't.

## Rebuilding from the ruins

If your partner has had an affair, you may feel gripped by the need to know every detail about the lover, while suffering the pain this causes when you are told. There is some evidence to suggest that if your questions are answered as fully and

truthfully as possible, you are more able to come to terms with what has happened eventually. If you were unfaithful, you might prefer not to talk about what happened, but once it is out in the open, you must respect your partner's right to know about it. It is much more possible for your partner to believe that you will not do it again if you are forthcoming about why it happened and what you felt. Making a new relationship together that is strong and happy means learning lessons from the affair about what was wrong before, so that you can both work to change the underlying causes.

The main casualty of a discovered affair is trust. When someone has been unfaithful to you once it may be hard to believe that it won't happen again. The cozy certainty that your partner would never do anything to hurt or deceive you has been shown to be false.

But couples who have successfully come through the trauma and found a new security together discover that there is a replacement for

### A fresh start

*Infidelity can make a couple feel there is no hope for the future, but if they both invest their all in making it work, there is a chance for a new, stronger relationship to emerge.*

simple trust. When both of you have been hurt and shaken by what has happened, and have looked at the possibility of parting and found it bleak, the decision to stay together takes on an entirely different meaning. You are able to say, "It won't happen again," not because you are incapable of being unfaithful, but because you have taken the conscious decision that you don't want to put your relationship at risk again.

When both of you recognize that for your relationship to survive happily *both* of you must try to make it more pleasant and workable, then you have an investment in making sure that neither of you knowingly causes the other pain.

# COPING WITH JEALOUSY

Jealousy is a perfectly natural emotion. When you are first in love, it is often an important feature of the relationship: You are so dazzled by the perfection of your partner that you can't believe your luck. There must be other people who think the same and want your partner for themselves, or your partner is so wonderful that perhaps you aren't good enough. Jealousy is also a normal reaction if your partner is attracted to someone else, flirts seriously with someone, or has an affair with or strong affection for someone else that excludes you.

Jealousy becomes a damaging emotion, however, when there is no special reason for it. When a person remains convinced that his or her partner is interested in someone else despite genuine denials and reassurances, or is sure that the partner is having an affair, wants to have an affair, or is bound to be unfaithful in the near future—against all evidence—then the jealousy is no longer a natural reaction. It is, instead, a personality trait with potentially destructive consequences.

## Damaging effects

Irrational jealously is usually the result of deep insecurity. People who are habitually jealous without cause have frequently had a childhood in which they often felt excluded or unloved, or in which love seemed to be traded for certain types of behavior. Children who lost a parent through death or who had only partial contact as a result of divorce, may also feel that loved ones cannot be relied on to stay around; this can translate into compulsive jealousy when they become adults.

Jealousy can be flattering initially. It makes a partner feel wanted and loved. But when it persists without cause it feels controlling, restrictive, and

***A distorted view***
*Jealousy colors your view, so that you regard everything your partner says or does with suspicion and distrust.*

unloving. Jealous people have a voracious need to know what their partners are doing at all times. They overreact to interest shown in others, or at the slightest suspicion that the intensity of the relationship is waning. They check up on their partner's whereabouts, make a scene, or punish the partner by becoming emotionally cold or sexually withdrawn.

In this way, jealousy becomes a self-fulfilling prophecy. The jealous behavior makes life a misery for the partner, and leads to the feared result.

## Conquering jealousy

Recognizing that jealousy stems from low self-esteem, fear of being unlovable, or a generalized sense that love is unreliable, is the first step. Making efforts to curtail jealous behavior is also important. When lack of trust or anger or coldness has started to affect your relationship, acting in a more trusting way, whether you feel it or not, starts to reverse the process. A partner who is treated well is more likely to take your feelings into account. It is worth making the effort to explain to your partner, at a time when you are not in the grip of jealousy, why you are sometimes driven to behave as you do. Letting your partner know how vulnerable you feel is likely to make him or her more understanding and more careful not to upset you. Anything you can do to increase your confidence and feelings of self-worth will contribute to putting your jealous feelings into proportion. Sometimes therapy or counseling can help you start the process.

If your partner is the jealous one, you must recognize that bolstering his or her self-esteem is necessary. Don't feel that your love can be taken for granted: show in words and gestures what you feel. You should also pay attention to the way you behave so that you don't hurt your partner unintentionally. Small considerations help, such as calling when you say you will, making an effort to be punctual, and not leaving your partner stranded at a party. But giving into irrational demands from a jealous partner will not help in the long-term. Indulging the behavior doesn't cure it: it just makes you feel more trapped and miserable. Ultimately, a compulsively jealous person must look inward for the reasons why he or she feels this way, and take responsibility for the behavior rather than looking to a partner to provide the cure.

# OPEN RELATIONSHIPS

In an open relationship, according to theory, both people are free to take other sexual partners. The couples may be committed but feel that sex in the long-term loses excitement. Short-term sex with someone new provides the missing ingredient.

In *Open Marriage—A New Life Style for Couples*, researchers George and Nena O'Neill spoke to 16 couples in open marriages and identified common factors in their success. The couple had to be well-balanced, secure, and independent, as did the sex partners, who had to understand that their relationships were secondary.

## A cause of conflict

For most people, however, this arrangement rarely works long-term. In *Marriage, Love, Sex and Divorce*, Jonathan Gathorne-Hardy interviewed Jane and Philip about their open marriage. Their story shows the weakness in the arrangement. During the first year, when one took a lover, the other felt he or she had to. This competitiveness results in bad feeling, particularly if one is more sexually active than the other.

Jane said, "With Philip it's libido; he has a greater need. Mine last longer. I definitely love two of them." This attitude causes problems for many couples. Love can threaten the couple's bond more than sex. When both partners feel happy, healthy, and confident it is easier to cope with an outsider. But when one of them goes through a bad patch, the lover can be a catalyst that exacerbates anxiety.

## Dangerous consequences

The threat of AIDS inevitably affects open relationships. Safe sex is incompatible with casual sexual freedom. Sensible and secure lovers, vital to an open relationship, are likely to be cautious about embarking on an affair with someone who has a history of sleeping around. You have to ask yourself if the pleasure is worth the risks. You also have to be sure that your love is strong enough to stand the strain. And is the dissatisfaction you feel purely sexual? Answers to these questions show whether an open relationship is a dangerous mixture that will harm a partnership rather than strengthen it.

# THE VITAL INGREDIENTS

DOES IT SOMETIMES SEEM as though everywhere you turn, you are confronted by increasingly depressing divorce-rate statistics? It appears that sustaining a relationship for a lifetime is an impossible dream. Yet you probably also know several couples who have not only stayed together for many years, but who actually seem still to like and love each other, to share interests and feelings, and to choose to spend time together rather than merely being with each other out of habit or simply fear of being alone.

So what is the secret of such couples' staying power? Perhaps you feel that they have just been lucky enough to find the right partner? Or that they are party to some secret formula for romantic success? In fact, there is no magic trick: the capacity to build a good and lasting relationship is something that almost anyone can learn.

## Why relationships fail
Counsellors experienced in helping couples through crises and problems in their relationships are generally agreed about the main reasons why people split up. Other things may cloud the issue—such as loss of interest in sex, lack of money, or rows about the children—but they are often symptoms or surface difficulties rather than fundamental causes. There are two particularly significant and destructive problems: One is a lack of good communication; the other is an inability to accept change and adapt to one another's fluctuating needs and desires.

## The foundation stones of success
Being aware of potential problems that can destroy relationships yields insights into how to build and sustain a good partnership. The key words are communication and flexibility. You cannot overestimate

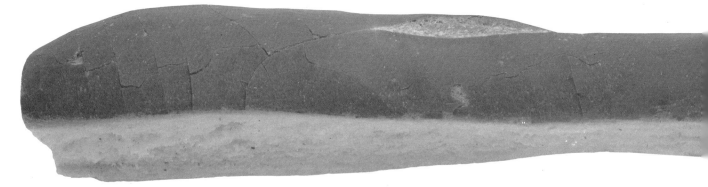

## A SATISFYING SANDWICH

Criticizing another person with positive results is always difficult, but it tends to be most explosive in your love relationship. For many people, criticism feels like attack, so their natural response is to go on the defensive. Unfortunately, if someone reacts like this, he or she is then unlikely to hear what is being said. Equally, fear of being hurtful may prevent the critic from expressing valid and honest feelings.

Learning how to handle criticism—giving or receiving it—is vital to the stability of a long-term relationship. When you find it necessary to offer criticism, make it clear that it is the deed you dislike, not the person. So if your partner tends to switch television channels without consultation, limit your criticism to this specific action. Similarly, never criticize in front of anyone else, since this will only cause antagonism and humiliation. Remember that if you want your partner to accept your remarks, you must make them palatable in some way.

## Building a relationship

*Together, you can build a solid and enduring relationship based on firm foundations—mutual understanding, effective communication, and a willingness to adapt to change.*

the value of talking. Talking keeps your interest in each other alive; it allows you to know and understand each other better; it helps prevent misunderstandings; it enables you to deal with problems before they become serious or deeply entrenched. Talking is free, and you can do it anywhere and anytime, yet most of us at some time in our lives avoid it like the plague. How much easier it seems to change the subject, walk out of the room, or assume that you know how the other person feels without needing to ask. But talking is the most crucial form of sharing in relationships: sharing

All of us find it easier to accept criticisms, and modify our behavior accordingly, if they are offered in a "sandwich" of positive points:
1) Say something positive: for example, "I love it when we have a cozy evening watching television." This will help prevent your partner from going on the defensive.
2) Make your specific criticism of the offending behavior: "But I do find it frustrating when you change channels without asking me if I was watching the original one. I feel you don't care what I think."

3) Follow up the criticism with another positive statement or feeling: "If we chat about what we both want to watch, we'll enjoy our viewing even more."

When you receive criticism, view it as an opportunity to improve your relationship, not as a personal attack. Ask your partner to construct his or her remarks in the way shown, then listen to what is being said rather than automatically denying or justifying your actions. Being able to give and take criticism will help you to grow together, and your relationship will benefit as a result.

your thoughts and feelings, your doubts and fears, your hopes and dreams, is one of the vital ingredients that keeps a relationship alive (see also "Are You Communicating?" pp. 78-81 and "The Art of Negotiation," pp. 100-103).

Flexibility is no less important. Keeping an open mind and a flexible attitude allows you to accept and welcome change—in yourself, in your partner, and in your relationship. Think back to the way you were when you were a child: Do you see yourself as the same person now only with a larger shoe size? Of course not. All people change as they progress through life and are affected by their various experiences.

## A change for the better

The process of change—of growing up and maturing—is never ending, and you need to be just as accommodating about changes in your partner and in your relationship as you are about yourself. Expecting your partner to remain the same as he or she was on the day you first met is unrealistic. A healthy relationship will naturally evolve as you both change over the years, and this will be a source of enormous satisfaction and strength, of greater closeness and love rather than a threat or a sign that you're no longer right for each other.

One of the most difficult areas for partners to get right is the balance between sharing their lives as a couple and leading fulfilling lives as individuals. There are no hard and fast rules for this— what works for one couple won't necessarily work for another. Many couples find that, particularly in the early stages of a relationship, their lives become so wrapped up in each other that they become mutually overdependent. There is nothing wrong with being one another's best friend and principal

### Staying in touch
*Showing someone you care for them with affectionate gestures and physical intimacy helps to sustain the bond between you.*

source of support—in fact, this is one of the great pleasures of being in a happy relationship; however, if you are each other's only source of support, you are likely to be putting on too much pressure and you may become set in a needy pattern.

No matter how close you are to your partner, always keep some time and space for yourself and your own needs, interests, and friends. As well as contributing to your sense of self-worth and your own identity, keeping your own friends and interests has benefits for you both as a couple: First, it helps you maintain a sense of proportion about minor worries, because your relationship is not the only important element in your life; second, it helps you replenish your mental reserves so you have more to offer the partnership and more to talk about— after all, if you do everything together, you may run short of things to say to each other. You are also likely to appreciate more, the time you do share, because you know you are sharing by choice, not out of habit or because your life holds no other interest for you.

## Physical laws

While it is natural for an individual's level of sexual desire to ebb and flow, and a couple's pattern of lovemaking to vary during the course of their relationship, it is extremely important for a couple to maintain physical affection and closeness with each other. Whenever possible, demonstrate your fondness openly with caring touches: a soothing massage when your partner is tense after a difficult time at work, a back scrub in the bath, gentle stroking of his or her hair, a comforting cuddle at the end of the day. Always take time to greet each other and say goodbye properly with a hug and a kiss rather than proffering your cheek for a cursory peck.

# THE RELATIONSHIPS CHARTER

While it is impossible to come up with a single magic formula that will guarantee the success of any relationship, there are some important points that, if followed, will benefit both partners, and provide a good basis for forging and maintaining a happy and sustainable partnership for many years.

## Talking

Talking is the cement that holds the structure of a relationship together. Talking allows you to make the most of your good times together, and helps you through misunderstandings, disagreements, and bad patches. It prevents problems from blowing out of proportion and defuses grievances before they cause real damage. It should be a top priority for all couples.

## Listening

Listening does not mean nodding occasionally and saying "Yes, dear." It does mean being genuinely interested in what the other person has to say, allowing your partner to express him or herself without interruption, and making sure you have understood by occasionally repeating what the other has said, using your own words.

## Respect

Your partner deserves at least the same level of respect that you would accord any other close friend. Familiarity does not entitle you to disregard the necessity for mutual respect. Showing respect includes such things as not humiliating or disparaging your partner in public, taking time to listen attentively (see above), and accepting your partner's right to have different opinions from your own.

## Reassurance and praise

When you have something good to say, say it. There is no need to be reticent about your appreciation in case this might "spoil" the other person. A couple is a kind of mutual fan club. This doesn't mean gushing over each other meaninglessly; it means showing, and saying, how highly you think of each other, particularly when you feel your partner could do with a boost. Let your partner know that you are with him or her out of choice, not habit. When he or she does something you like or has made a special effort to look good, show your pleasure and appreciation.

## Loyalty

Do not criticize or rebuke your partner in public. This does not mean that you have to agree with each other all the time—just that you should not put your partner down or ridicule his or her point of view. When you do agree, be supportive. If someone else criticizes your partner personally (not just his or her opinions), you should provide strong back-up.

## Adaptability

You both need to be adaptable, to accommodate changes in your circumstances as well as changes in each other. You also have to accept that you don't necessarily both tackle things in the same way. This is important in small, everyday matters as well as in more fundamental concerns. For example, if your partner prepares vegetables in a different way from you but they still taste nice, then why try to make him or her prepare them your way? There is always more than one way of doing anything and other ways are not necessarily inferior—just different. Try to enjoy the fact that you do things differently, rather than seeing it as a cause of irritation.

# THE ART OF NEGOTIATION

It is a very unusual relationship in which there is never a clash of interests, or an occasion when one person wants one thing and the other is adamant that he or she wants something else. The way you handle these differences can make an enormous impact: not being heard or not listening to your partner are both dangerous. Either form of communication breakdown can dent your happiness severely, or even threaten your relationship.

## Finding a compromise

When you and your partner reach such an impasse, the most direct way forward is to meet each other halfway by finding a workable compromise. In some cases, this type of resolution is fairly easy to work out. When Mary and Paul won a large sum of money in a lottery, for example, their initial excitement was soon spoiled by a heated row about how the money should be spent. Mary, who put great store by financial security, felt strongly that they should use it for a major home-improvement program that included a new kitchen and bathroom. In complete contrast, Paul argued that the money represented a unique chance for them to fulfill their lifelong dream of traveling around the world. He saw Mary's plan as boring and materialistic, and couldn't bear to relinquish what he saw as their only chance of making such a trip.

The turning point for Paul and Mary came when they took the time to understand one another's point of view; Paul took into account that Mary's need for security stemmed from her unstable family background, while Mary realized that Paul's dreamy nature was one of the things that attracted her to him. Once they had reached this stage, they were able to find a middle path: they used part of the money to do work on the house, and the rest for an extended holiday that included some of the places they both wanted to see.

### Taking the strain

*Couples often find themselves pulling needlessly against one another when it comes to making decisions within a relationship. Although everyone has arguments occasionally, there are ways of lessening the combative nature of major differences of opinion.*

Beth and Conor faced a similar standoff, but their situation caused considerable friction every weekend. Conor, who was part of a close family, always went home for Sunday lunch. Beth found this hard to understand, since the members of her own family hardly ever got together, so although Conor took her with him on his visits, she resented the regular loss of so much of their limited free time. Instead of having the same argument over and over again, they reached a compromise that suited them both. They agreed to see Conor's family every other Sunday so they could spend alternate weekends alone together.

Unfortunately, some disagreements cannot be resolved in this way, either because the problem does not lend itself to compromise, or the partners cannot agree. When this happens, there are three useful tactics you can employ: making a list of benefits and disadvantages on both sides, switching roles and arguing one another's viewpoint, and consulting an objective arbitrator.

### Hot tickets

*Many disagreements can be resolved by reaching a compromise. When a couple are unable to decide between a practical or frivolous answer to a problem, then a solution that encompasses both should perhaps be sought.*

## Listing the pros and cons

Simply writing down the consequences of both courses of action can often bring things clearly into focus. When Nick was offered a much better job in a far-flung city, his wife Leonie asked him to turn it down. She wanted to stay where they were because she had grown up in the area and her family and friends, as well as her job, were all close by. Because he had no such ties, Nick was strongly in favor of the change, and felt sure they would both benefit from the increased opportunities the offer gave him. To get beyond this impasse, Nick and Leonie took it in turn to write down everything they would gain by moving and everything they

would gain by staying. Then they wrote out the disadvantages in each case. This exercise allowed them to view their choices more clearly, away from the emotionally loaded atmosphere of an argument. Once Nick looked dispassionately at the number and strength of Leonie's reasons for wanting to stay, he agreed to turn down the offer, and look for a better job nearby.

## Switching roles

Another useful technique, and one that is often suggested by relationship counsellors, is a form of role playing in which each partner argues the other's case instead of his or her own. This not only helps each to understand the opposing view, it also allows both partners to make sure their own has been understood accurately.

Graham and June, like many other couples, could not plan their annual vacation without fighting. While they were both single, Graham was so involved in his job that he never took any time off,

and June went away alone or with a girlfriend. After they were married, however, June expected this to change, while Graham wanted the arrangements to stay exactly the same. Examining the other point of view thoroughly enough to present it was a revelation to both partners. Graham had not realized how hurt and rejected June felt by his refusal to spend any vacation time with her; she perceived time spent together this way as an essential part of being married. For her part, June had never appreciated the pressure Graham was under at work, or the depth of his fears of unemployment. Once these misunderstandings were cleared up, both partners felt more secure, and were able to give a little. Now, they take one brief, relaxing holiday together, and June books a longer, more active break without Graham.

## Wise counsel

When two people cannot agree, professional counseling (as opposed to analysis or therapy, which are much more complex) is often the answer. The role of a counselor is not to make decisions for you, but to help you work out your own feelings, and communicate with each other in a clear and focused way. Your family doctor may be able to recommend a local organization or individual.

Jake, for example, tended to collapse in front of the television when he came home from work, whereas his wife Kate, who had been at home all day with two young children, was desperate for adult conversation. The more angry Kate became with Jake, the more surly and silent he became; each felt the other was being demanding and selfish. In their counseling sessions, they were encouraged to talk together without hurling accusations or throwing up defenses. Like all effective negotiating techniques, counseling worked by helping both parties understand and appreciate one another's needs.

### Different destinations

*Even potentially pleasant tasks, such as planning a holiday, can result in disagreement. It is important for both parties in a relationship to understand the other's needs so that a mutually pleasing solution can be reached.*

# THE ART OF GIVE AND TAKE

Are you pig-headed and always determined to get your way? Or are you the first to put your own needs on hold and give in to another's wishes? Alternatively, perhaps you can ask for what you want but are prepared to compromise or give way when necessary. Being able to give and take is extremely important in a relationship, but many people find it difficult to ask clearly for what they want from a partner, or they just take what they want without regard for the partner's feelings and needs.

In *The Relate Guide to Starting Again* by Sarah Litvinoff, there is an exercise that helps you to identify the typical pattern of the way you deal with give and take, so you can see where you should make changes if there is an imbalance.

Cast your mind back to when you were a child. Imagine that you are with several other children and you are offered in turn a plate of mixed biscuits, beginning with you. There is only one chocolate biscuit and you want it, but what do you do?

• Would you say: "I don't mind, let the others choose first," even though you do mind, really? Perhaps you were taught always to put others before yourself. As an adult, being liked is more important to you than having what you want. This can make you unhappy in a relationship because you probably expect your partner to guess what you want.

• Would you say: "I'd like the plain biscuit," then eat it without enjoyment? If so, you are a martyr. You tend to expect others to notice or anticipate your needs without your expressing them clearly, and when they do not, you feel aggrieved.

• Would you grab the chocolate biscuit and eat it quickly before anyone notices it was the only one? If so, you assume that everyone feels the same as you and wants the same things. As an adult, you might be irritated by others' needs because you think that if you meet them your own desires will not be attended to. And you will be oblivious to signals from a partner who does not ask for things directly.

*Patterns of behavior*
*By looking at how you behaved during an apparently innocuous childhood situation, such as choosing a biscuit, it may be possible to see how these youthful patterns have affected your adult attitudes.*

• Would you say: "I want the chocolate one, but if anyone else wants it I'll have it next time." This shows that you are able to say what you want and give way to another, while ensuring that you get what you want another time. You recognize that others have desires as strong as your own and you are prepared to put your needs on hold for the sake of good relations.

This last response is the most balanced. If you can give way to another's needs, confident in the belief that to do so is not to sacrifice your own needs, you have learned the art of give and take.

# MANAGING CHANGE

As time passes, all people change—in response to their personal experiences, their relationships with other people, and the environments in which they live and work. In general, these changes take place at a fairly slow pace, which makes it relatively easy for partners, friends, and family to accept and adjust gradually to them. Where changes are much more sudden or fundamental, however, they can alter the basic structure of a relationship quite dramatically, and often cause serious problems as a result. The birth of a first child frequently has this effect, as does sudden unemployment or, conversely, a significant promotion or a new, high-powered job. Other potentially difficult times occur when someone retires, becomes seriously ill or incapacitated, gains or loses a significant amount of weight, or experiences a bereavement.

## Why is change so threatening?

When we are children, our sense of security is created largely by the familiar, stable elements of our lives: Getting up at the same time each morning, watching the same TV programs, playing the same sport on the same day each week. When such comforting routines are broken for some reason, it can create a disproportionate sense of alarm, and a fear that our whole way of life is under threat.

Adult life, however, requires a certain degree of flexibility: If there is a train strike, you travel on the bus; when a colleague is off sick, you take on extra work to help out. Most people cope with this type of situation very well, but from time to time disruptions occur that cause acute anxiety, and bring back all the childhood insecurities.

The most unsettling changes are those that render you a passive victim of their effects, even though you were not the instigator. For example, if your partner decided to retrain for a new career, or study for a higher qualification, he or she would probably feel very positive about taking such a step. However, you might resent the resulting loss of income, or even fear that you will be left behind in some way: your partner might become increasingly ambitious or educated and as a result will become bored with you.

If, however, you know that your partner still loves you despite obtaining a degree, becoming absorbed in a new baby, or losing a lot of weight, then you will find the changes much less threatening: what most people fear is not the change itself, but the losses that may result. Similarly, people worry that when someone close to them makes one enormous life change, more might be on the way. If a partner who once expressed no interest in education, for example, suddenly becomes a prize scholar, will he also decide he no longer wants you?

Expressing your fears openly can do a great deal toward diminishing them. At the same time—if you're the one changing—it's important to

*Moving on*
*A major turning point such as a house move can make you feel apprehensive and unsure of the future—even if it is ultimately a change for the better.*

**Settling in**
*Fear of impending change is often simply a fear of the unknown. It tends to melt away when you begin to get used to a new place or situation, and realize that it is an improvement.*

acknowledge that any major changes you are contemplating may have an unsettling effect on those around you, so you should take care to offer reassurance as well as seeking it.

Another important aspect of change is that even when it is positive and exciting, such as moving to a better neighborhood, it can still be difficult because it carries with it a sense of separation and loss. On the surface, it may seem odd to mourn a cramped apartment when you move to a three-bedroom house in the suburbs, but what you are really mourning is a part of you and your life that is disappearing forever. What's more, you may fear moving to a new place because it is unknown; even if you were not happy in your old apartment, you will miss the comfort of familiar surroundings.

Because all individuals are constantly growing and developing, their relationships cannot stay the same, and this process of change—sudden or gradual—may feel very frightening. There will always be times when you don't know how to behave, or even how to feel with a partner, a parent, or a close friend. But, like all emotional problems, if you can work through these changes with the people closest to you, you will achieve stronger, deeper relationships as a result.

## THE RELATIONSHIP AND US

Professional counselors often talk about a relationship as a separate entity. There is "you," there is "me," and then there is "us." The "us" element is more than a combination of the two, however—it is something extra you create together. So while in a relationship you may both do certain things solely for yourselves, there are other things you do especially for the relationship.

Write down the ways in which you and your partner contribute to your life together. For example, it may be that both of you are very involved in your careers, and if you were single, you would put in very long hours. But, as a couple, you both realize that you need to spend time doing things together—seeing friends, watching films, or just talking quietly. For the sake of the relationship, you both sacrifice your immersion in your respective careers in order to maintain communication with one another.

In the same way, you might organize regular vacations with your partner even though neither of you is particularly interested in travel; making time for each other in this way will improve your relationship. Try to think of other ways in which, by treating your relationship as a separate entity, you can nourish it and help it to grow and thrive.

**United we stand...**
*A relationship is a new entity, drawing from both partners without diminishing them.*

# MAKE ROOM FOR GROWTH

A close, nurturing emotional relationship is one of the most important elements of a healthy, fulfilling life. At its best, it provides a firm and loving base from which both partners can not only function, but grow, flourish, and branch out in all directions. For this to happen, though, it's important for each partner to allow the other enough emotional space to develop as an individual. You need room to nurture your career or other talents. You must also be tolerant of your partner's wanting to engage in some activities separately. In healthy relationships, each partner allows the other time apart. At the very least, this gives them something to talk about besides work and their children. If you have nothing that takes you away from each other, apart from work, then you will not develop as individuals and neither will the relationship.

### Separate interests

*Although you should feel happy and contented sharing time and interests with your partner, it is vital to find and maintain your own identity outside your relationship.*

For example, Jill and Peter were so wrapped up in each other that they dropped all their former friends and interests. Eventually, their relationship became so insular that it was increasingly difficult for each to cope with a social function unless the other one was also there. This over-reliance on each other stopped them from growing and developing as separate individuals. And it put a huge strain on the marriage, as neither of them had anyone else to share their worries and their woes with. In addition, excluding their friends in this way made many of those friends feel puzzled and hurt.

## Getting the balance right

Time spent alone and time spent with other people is actually just as valuable to your relationship as time spent together. However, couples who spend too much time apart tend to grow apart. It's all a question of balance. So it is important to integrate some of your outside activities with the relationship. For example, if you belong to a sports club, allow your partner to feel involved by inviting him or her along occasionally to attend social functions or just to watch what's going on. Likewise, if your partner has an interest in a leisure pursuit that you do not share, go along sometimes and join in.

# INTERDEPENDENCE

Healthy relationships always involve a recognition that as well as a certain measure of dependence upon each other, there is some independence maintained after the relationship has been established. This is known as interdependence.

### Lean on me
*Within any relationship there are times when you have to support one another. But it is important that the supporting role isn't the domain of only one person or the relationship might overbalance.*

## Supporting each other

At times you will feel very dependent upon your partner. For example, after losing a job, after the birth of a child, or following a personal crisis, you may feel very needy and want a lot of support and comfort. At times like these your partner is, or should be, your rock. He or she represents a safe place for you to seek comfort in when the world around you appears both frightening and hostile.

Likewise, there will be times when life outside the relationship is difficult for your partner. Perhaps he or she faces a difficulty within his or her family or at work. Or perhaps he or she is ill. There will also be difficult times for both of you when your strength will derive from a sense of togetherness—of having an ally by your side. Working through difficult times together can make both of you much stronger.

You will probably find yourselves taking it in turns to be the strong one. And after an episode in which you have been the one needing support, it is tremendously satisfying to give support in return. Healthy couples take turns like this without even thinking about it.

### Changing roles

Sometimes it is much harder for one partner to say he needs help, especially if he has tended to adopt the more supportive role in the relationship. If this is the case in your relationship, try to encourage your partner to share every aspect of his life with you—the bad as well as the good. For when one partner feels he is never allowed to be the more vulnerable, needy one, or to play a strong, supportive role, resentment can begin to breed beneath the surface.

The only way to ensure that your needs are met and that you in turn meet your partner's needs is to make sure you never stop communicating with each other.

When Melanie first met her husband George, he was a railway enthusiast: he adored spending every weekend traveling along old rail tracks on beautifully restored steam engines. Melanie had no interest in old trains but she did not wish to stop George from pursuing his love of them. Eventually, she went along on one of his trips out of curiosity, and she enjoyed it so much that the couple now spend most weekends together this way.

## Claustrophobic care

Conversely, Janine's partner Steve tried to discourage any interests she had outside their relationship. Steve did not like her to see any of the friends she had made before she met him. Nor did he want her to continue with her exercise and dance classes. Steve felt very threatened by any outside interest that Janine pursued, although he wanted to maintain contact with his former friends, especially his drinking pals. Janine loved Steve very much but she felt stifled by his possessiveness. She pointed out that it was no threat to their happiness if she kept up with her own friends. Steve admitted he was jealous of any outside interests she had because his first wife had used similar situations as a cover for an affair.

*__Moving on together__*
*If your partner develops interests outside your relationship it doesn't mean that you will be left behind—you should be able to appreciate the other person's enjoyment and progress together.*

Discovering why Steve felt so frightened by the fact that she had her own social life made Janine feel much less stifled by his possessiveness. To try and allay his fears, she introduced him to some of her old friends and arranged for them all to go out together occasionally. Gradually, Steve was able to accept that Janine was not using her outside interests as a cover for infidelity as his first wife had done, and that she was perfectly entitled to a social circle of her own, apart from the one she shared quite happily with him. Eventually, he felt confident enough to stop trying to prevent her from going out without him. Had he not done so, his relationship with Janine would have, at best, become stifled, claustrophic, and full of resentment. At worst, Janine would have left him for someone more tolerant and trusting.

## Trusting one another

Trust is the essential element that allows couples to continue to function as two individuals as well as a pair. Some couples feel able to take this trust to the very limit. For example, in addition to their annual break together, Jane and Derek always take a separate holiday with their own friends. Many people they know consider this strange, but they both feel that taking a holiday with their same-sex friends gives them a chance to remember their carefree youth when adult responsibilities, such as being married, earning a living, and paying bills were far off in the future.

One important factor in the success of their arrangement, however, is the fact that Jane and Derek trust each other implicitly because they understand that separate holidays are not a licence to be unfaithful—simply a chance to feel and behave, temporarily, like eight-year-olds again. Both return from these separate holidays refreshed and relaxed, but also very glad to be reunited.

## Growing together

There is no right or wrong way to pursue growth within your relationship. It is up to each individual couple to realize that growth and change should not be damaging and to look in detail at their own situation and work out what direction suits them best: what works for one couple will not necessarily work for another.

# FREEDOM TOGETHER

In his best-selling book *The Road Less Travelled*, M. Scott Peck, a leading American psychiatrist, claims that the highest form of relationship goes beyond romantic love. For couples to find true love, they must accept that they are both individuals and not be dependent on each other. Peck says that respect for each other's individuality is the only foundation upon which a mature relationship can be based.

## Giving love

Peck discusses the importance of caring for one another's spiritual growth. In order to do this, it is necessary to see love as an act of giving, rather than taking. It is a common misconception, he says, to believe that in order to love you must be dependent upon your spouse. He believes that such dependency actually crushes love. It is not love, but parasitism. For if you think you must have another individual for your survival, there is no choice and no freedom: the pairing is a matter of necessity. Two people love each other only when they are capable of living without each other and choose to live together.

To achieve a real sense of togetherness with someone you love, it is important that you let your loved one go, metaphorically speaking, and that, in turn, he or she lets you go. It is this act of letting go that—paradoxically—serves to bind a couple together even more strongly.

***Flying free***
*Freedom within a relationship is essential to its survival.*

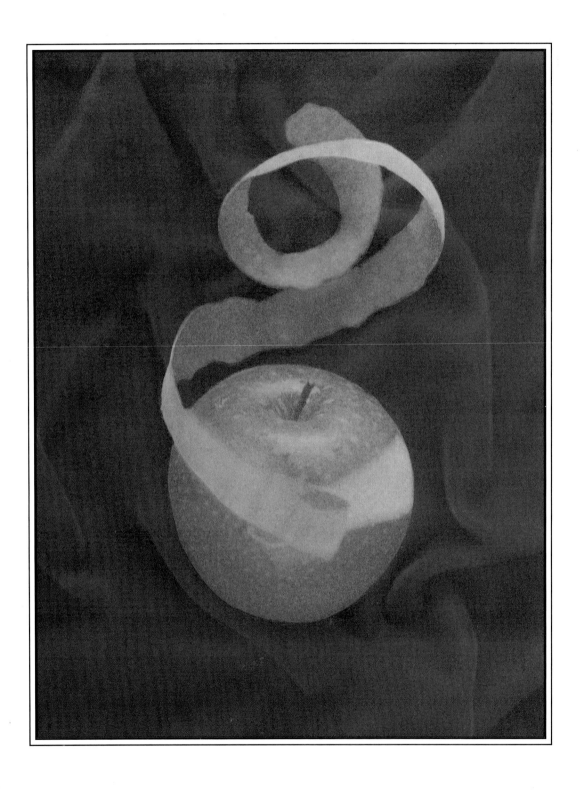

# CHAPTER FOUR

# SEX MATTERS

DOES SEX MATTER TO YOU? Have you ever wished you knew more about sex, or wanted to talk openly to your partner, but felt too embarrassed? Surprisingly, in an age when we are bombarded by sexual imagery in the form of films and videos, television, advertising, pop music, and magazines, many people still lack confidence in this vital area.

Chapter Four will help you expand your own sexual knowledge, and enable you to discover more about your partner's sexual beliefs and desires. It looks at the different ways in which men and women experience sexuality, and explores the sensitive subject of sexual technique, or being "good in bed." In this area, a vicious circle can easily be set up in which you feel embarrassed to talk to friends about sex, and so remain unsure about your sexual ability. You may then fear discussing sex with your partner in case your fragile self-confidence is damaged, and therefore never discover what you both really enjoy.

Couples starting out together often assume that their sex life will be natural and spontaneous, that change will be handled with ease, and that worries that beset others will never affect them. In fact, sex needs as much discussion as finance or child care. To help you open the channels of communication, this chapter includes four revealing questionnaires: "Test Your Sexual Knowledge," "Are You Sexually Satisfied?," "What's Your Sexual Style?," and "Are You Sexually Compatible?" Completing them individually, and then discussing your responses together honestly, will help you and your partner to become more open about your sexual desires and preferences.

Although most people's sex lives can be helped by making relatively simple changes and by communicating more freely, there are some sexual problems that need specific help. Difficulties such as premature ejaculation, or lack of orgasm, usually respond well to specialist advice and simple exercises advised by a sex therapist. If your sex life has become drearily familiar or predictable, then following some of the ideas and tips given in "When the Chemistry Changes" (see pp. 136-137) will help you reinvigorate this important part of your relationship.

The ability to talk together about sex will not only help you and your partner to negotiate the ups and downs of your physical relationship; good sexual communication can also transform the whole of your partnership for the better.

SEXUAL HAPPINESS LIES AT THE CORE OF EVERY SUCCESSFUL RELATIONSHIP, SO SHED YOUR INHIBITIONS AND ACCEPT THAT COMMUNICATION AND OPENNESS ARE VITAL TO SEXUAL FULFILLMENT.

# TEST YOUR SEXUAL KNOWLEDGE

MANY PEOPLE think they know all they need to know about sex, yet this vital area of information is often clouded with myths and misinformation. Separating fact from popular fiction, however, is an important step toward forming satisfying, sexual relationships. While few people would claim that sexual pleasure depends solely on having a high degree of knowledge, knowing fundamental facts about sex helps you avoid damaging preconceptions and free yourself of unnecessary insecurity.

Read through the following questions and, for each one, choose the answer you think is correct. When you've finished, turn to page 139 to find the solutions—you may have a few surprises in store.

**1. What is the average age at which young people have sexual intercourse for the first time?**
**a)** 19   **b)** 17   **c)** 22

**2. Once a man's penis has become engorged and erect, is it important for him to go on to ejaculate?**
**a)** Yes, otherwise he runs the risk of physical harm. In addition, his erection can take a long time to subside and will feel extremely uncomfortable.
**b)** Yes, because if he allows the erection to go down, he will feel frustrated, or even angry with his partner.
**c)** No, it's perfectly normal for a man to have erections without ejaculating. This causes no physical harm to either the penis or the testicles.

**3. What is the earliest physical sign of sexual excitement in a woman?**
**a)** A flush that spreads over the upper body.
**b)** Wetness in the vagina.
**c)** Erect nipples.

**4. How many times each week does the average couple make love?**
**a)** Three or four times.
**b)** The frequency varies with the age of the couple and the length of the relationship.
**c)** Approximately once a week.

**5. Which group is likely to be the most promiscuous?**
**a)** Young single men.
   **b)** Middle-aged men.
      **c)** Young single women.

# UNDERSTANDING YOUR DIFFERENCES

On the whole, people of both sexes know more about male sexuality than female sexuality. This is probably because male sexuality is less complex, and its manifestations are largely external. Recently, however, research has led to a greater understanding of how women's bodies react during sex. Understanding these reactions and how they differ from those of men can lead to greatly increased pleasure for both partners.

One vital difference is in the way men and women react to touch. A man tends to initiate sex with the direct genital stimulation he enjoys, whereas a woman is more likely to respond to kisses and gentle caresses all over her body. As she becomes more aroused, the walls of her vagina begin to secrete lubrication, which some men mistakenly interpret as a sign of readiness for penetration. In fact, most women require a preliminary period of stimulation to the clitoris— their primary organ of sexual sensation. If this stops too soon, many women not only fail to climax, they also lose their sensation of arousal altogether. Continued stimulation, however, eventually leads to a strong urge for penetration; inside, the vagina enlarges and lengthens, and the woman is ready for orgasm.

During orgasm, the entrance to the vagina contracts rhythmically, and she experiences waves of intense pleasure. Unlike men, some women can climax several times in succession, but a short rest is sometimes necessary after each one since the clitoris is too sensitive then for even gentle touch.

In general, a woman's sexual responses are triggered by different stimuli from those of a man, and they are more dependent on closeness and affection. Certainly, women who feel relaxed with their partner are more likely to enjoy sex and achieve orgasm.

*Patterns of pleasure*
*Women (pink) take longer than men (blue) to respond sexually, but their responses last longer.*

**6. Does the clitoris stay visible during sex?**
**a)** Yes, because it becomes erect like a man's penis.
**b)** No, it is on show only until the woman becomes fully aroused, then it retracts under a fold of skin at the top of the vaginal lips.
**c)** No, it's too small to see.

**7. Do women prefer large penises?**
**a)** Yes, because a large penis is able to stimulate the vagina more effectively.
**b)** No—the walls of a woman's vagina are elastic, so they can be stimulated by a penis of any size.

**8. A woman cannot be sexually fulfilled unless she achieves regular orgasms.**
**a)** True: orgasms are a basic and fundamental part of sex.

**b)** False: many women find sex satisfying and enjoyable even without an orgasm.

**9. Homosexual men always have anal sex when they make love.**
**a)** True: homosexual men have to do this in order to achieve ejaculation.
**b)** False: anal sex is only one of a wide range of homosexual practices.

**10. To prevent himself from ejaculating too soon, a man should try to focus his mind on something mundane, such as a squash game or a shopping list.**
**a)** False: this technique can actually raise anxiety, and lead to premature ejaculation.
**b)** True: this simple technique is often very effective.

# ARE YOU SEXUALLY SATISFIED?

THIS QUIZ WILL HELP YOU explore your level of satisfaction with your sexual relationship. Decide which of the answers best describes your current relationship, or most closely resembles the patterns established with previous partners.

**1. How often do you make love?**
**a)** Often enough to satisfy my needs.
**b)** Slightly too often, or not quite often enough.
**c)** Not nearly enough, or far too frequently.

**2. Where do you make love?**
**a)** Wherever we both feel comfortable.
**b)** Usually where my partner suggests, but occasionally I express another preference.
**c)** I always go along with my partner, but I often feel uncomfortable and unhappy.

**3. When do you make love?**
**a)** Any time, according to how we both feel.
**b)** Usually when my partner is in the mood, but once in a while when it suits me.
**c)** When my partner wants to.

**4. Who initiates sex?**
**a)** Either of us, depending on the situation.
**b)** It's usually the same person, but the other almost always agrees to go ahead.
**c)** Nearly always just one of us.

**5. How awkward do you find the lead-up to your lovemaking?**
**a)** I am comfortable with how this happens.
**b)** Our normal pattern usually works well, but I would like to break it sometimes.
**c)** I always feel extremely frustrated and resentful, either because I generally have to make the first move, or because my partner never wants me to do this.

**6. How do you let your partner know you want to make love?**
**a)** We communicate clearly with words or touches.
**b)** I sometimes ask, but it normally develops from a cuddle.
**c)** It's embarrassing to ask—it has to be spontaneous.

**7. Do you and your partner feel the same way about planning ahead to make love?**
**a)** Yes, this is not a problem for us.
**b)** I usually follow my partner's lead, but occasionally I express a different view.
**c)** No, I am unhappy, either because my partner insists on setting aside specific times for sex and I find this destroys spontaneity, or because I'd like to anticipate sex, but my partner refuses to make plans in advance.

**8. Are you and your partner equally comfortable with your own and each other's nakedness?**
**a)** Yes, we both feel the same way about it.
**b)** Nakedness or obvious concealment occasionally make me feel slightly awkward.
**c)** No, my partner's feelings are very different from mine, and this makes me feel very uncomfortable.

**9. Are you able to touch your partner in a way that suits you both?**
**a)** Yes, my caresses are pleasurable for both of us.
**b)** Not always, I am occasionally uncomfortable with what my partner wants.
**c)** No, my partner either wants to be touched in a way that I dislike, or objects to being touched in a way that I enjoy.

**10. Are you satisfied with the length of time you spend on foreplay?**
**a)** Yes, our foreplay is perfectly satisfactory.
**b)** Occasionally I would like it to go on longer or stop sooner.
**c)** No, I am always unhappy because foreplay stops too soon or takes much too long.

**11. Does your partner's touch give you pleasure?**
**a)** Yes, my partner can be gentle or firm depending on my particular desire at the time.
**b)** Mostly, but sometimes I find that he or she can be a bit insensitive.
**c)** No, my partner doesn't have any idea about how I would really like to be touched.

**12. Do you find it easy to talk to your partner while you are making love?**
**a)** Yes, I regularly discuss my feelings quite openly and ask for my needs to be met.
**b)** I do talk about our relationship, but I find it difficult to discuss anything sexual.
**c)** No, I am too embarrassed.

**13. How do you decide what the level of lighting should be during lovemaking?**
**a)** We change the atmosphere to suit our feelings. Sometimes we like to make love in the dark, other times we create a more sensual mood using candles or soft lighting.
**b)** We usually make love by the same light, and occasionally I would like a change.
**c)** Because my partner feels strongly about this, we always make love in the same level of light. I feel very uncomfortable with this, but go along anyway.

**14. If you don't feel like sex, can you say so?**
**a)** Yes, my partner and I are both able to do this.
**b)** Usually, although I sometimes go ahead with sex to please my partner even though I don't feel like it .
**c)** No, my partner would be very hurt or angry so I always say yes to keep the peace.

**15. If a problem arises during lovemaking (like loss of erection) are you able to solve it?**
**a)** Yes, we can talk about it reasonably openly.
**b)** Sometimes I feel too shy to discuss it.
**c)** No, problems get swept under the carpet, only to surface again the next time.

**16. Are you and your partner always able to reconcile your expectations of lovemaking?**

**a)** Yes, sometimes we end up just kissing and cuddling rather than having intercourse, but there is never any conflict about it.

**b)** Usually. When my partner's needs are different from mine, I tend to go along.

**c)** No, my partner always seems to demand sex when I just want a cuddle, or vice versa.

**17. Do you and your partner feel the same about stimulating each other manually?**

**a)** Yes, we both enjoy this part of lovemaking.

**b)** Not always. I would like a little more, or less, of this kind of stimulation.

**c)** No, our expectations are completely different, and this causes enormous problems.

**18. Do you and your partner both share the same attitude to oral sex?**

**a)** Yes, we are completely compatible in this area.

**b)** Not always. I would like my partner to take more account of my wishes.

**c)** No, our desires and expectations are completely different, which causes frustration and tension.

**19. Do you like to use sexy magazines or videos as part of your sexual relationship?**

**a)** We both find this kind of visual stimulation arousing, and I feel satisfied with our present level of use.

**b)** Once in a while. One of other of us is more keen on them and tends to suggest it.

**c)** No, either I would like to experiment with this or my partner is keen but I dislike the idea.

**20. Would you like to experience either anal stimulation or intercourse?**

**a)** We are satisfied with the level of anal arousal we have in our lovemaking.

**b)** We have tried this, but one or other of us enjoys it more.

**c)** No: either I would like to find out if it is arousing and my partner isn't at all willing, or my partner is keen but I don't feel happy with the idea.

**21. Do you normally have a chance to use your favorite positions for sex?**

**a)** Yes, we both enjoy making love in a variety of positions.

**b)** I don't usually have much choice when it comes to choosing what position we adopt.

**c)** No, my partner likes sex only in one position, and I tend to go along with this.

**22. Is sexual fantasy part of your foreplay?**

**a)** Yes, we often share intimate fantasies.

**b)** I do have fantasies, but I could never tell my partner because he or she would be upset.

**c)** No, I'm afraid my partner would feel jealous if the fantasy were not about him or her.

**23. How do you feel about using an aid to arousal, such as a vibrator?**

**a)** My partner and I would both be interested.

**b)** I'm a bit doubtful; it sounds too mechanical.

**c)** Either my partner would strongly object, and think I am implying that he or she is a bad lover, or my partner likes the idea but I am not keen.

**24. Are there other sexual areas you would like to experience, such as bondage, dressing up, sex in groups, etc.?**

**a)** I could discuss these things with my partner, but would respect his or her decision whatever it may be.

b) I do feel curious about these sometimes, but wouldn't discuss it with my partner.
c) My partner and I have very different views about sexual experimentation, but don't discuss it.

### 25. What do you do after lovemaking?
a) I like to lie in my partner's arms and relax. We both think this is part of lovemaking.
b) My partner tends to roll over and go to sleep, or leap up to make a cup of tea. I would like him or her to relax more.
c) Nothing; I often feel rejected.

### 26. If you raised the subject of sex outside of lovemaking, would you be able to talk easily?
a) Yes, we can discuss sexual matters easily.
b) It can be difficult—it seems unnatural outside of bed. I would value more openness.
c) No, it would probably end up in a row. I would like to be able to talk more easily.

### 27. How does your partner feel about the idea of your masturbating and what do you think about this?
a) I feel able to masturbate without feeling my partner disapproves. I am comfortable with this side of my sexuality.
b) My partner tends to see it as a criticism of him or her. I often feel guilty about this side of me.
c) My partner cannot cope with the idea of my masturbating, so I don't do it. I would like to be able to do this.

### 28. Would you like to watch your partner masturbate?
a) Yes, we have tried this, and it excites me.
b) Maybe, but I don't think my partner would feel comfortable with this idea.
c) Yes, this idea really appeals to me, but I'm sure my partner would never agree.

### 29. Would you like to be watched while you masturbate?
a) Yes, we have tried this and both find it arousing.
b) Yes, this appeals to me, but my partner might not agree.
c) Maybe, but my partner would probably be horrified if I ever suggested such a prospect.

### 30. In general terms, do you feel satisfied with your sexual relationship?
a) Yes, it helps to bond our relationship, and I feel pleased with most parts of it.
b) Sometimes. I would like more openness and experimentation in my sex life.
c) No, it rarely meets my needs, and can cause much unhappiness between us.

• *For conclusions, see page 140.*

# EXPRESSING YOUR NEEDS CLEARLY

Can you express your needs clearly? When you're faced with asking your boss for more money, or approaching a neighbor about excessive noise, it's all too easy to create bad feeling. So it's hardly surprising that when it comes to asking for their sexual needs to be met, many people feel nervous and inadequate. Often it seems easier to stay silent, even though this may mean missing out on a greater level of sexual satisfaction.

## The real world

One major difficulty is that people often expect their partners to know intuitively what they want without being told. This idealistic view of sex—that people in love should be so naturally in tune that discussion is unnecessary—is unrealistic. Healthy sexual relationships require communication and negotiation, not only to succeed in the first place, but also to meet each person's changing needs. A young couple, for example, may have very different sexual needs after the birth of a child. If the relationship is to survive, they must acknowledge and explore these changes, and express clearly what they want from one another.

Unfortunately, assertiveness and plain speaking are often confused with aggression, or demanding your own way at the expense of others. In fact, being assertive involves saying clearly and openly what you want without putting the other person in the wrong. At a later stage, you may have to compromise, but stating clearly how you feel at the outset puts any subsequent negotiations on a much stronger footing.

To familiarize yourself with the way assertiveness works, read the following scenarios and compare the different unassertive responses with the assertive ones:

**Scenario 1:** Clare has been going out with Marcus for three weeks. Although they have kissed and cuddled, they have not yet made love. Clare is still unsure of the relationship and does not feel ready for sex. One evening, Marcus attempts a degree of intimacy that Clare finds uncomfortable.
**1.** Clare pushes Marcus away, and shouts, "How dare you! Don't ever try that again!"
**2.** Clare suddenly gets up, mumbling, "You have to go now—I've got to get up early in the morning."
**3.** Clare begins to cry. When Marcus asks her what's wrong, she replies, "Nothing."

**Assertive response**: Clare gently pushes Marcus away, and says "I really like you, but I'm not ready to make love. I want to know you a little better first."

**Scenario 2:** Lisa and Penny have been together for a year. Lisa would like Penny to massage her back as a preamble to lovemaking, but she never seems to do it.
**1.** Lisa shouts angrily, "What's wrong with you?—I've asked you a hundred times to rub my back."
**2.** Lisa asks coyly, "Can you remember what I asked for last week?"
**3.** Lisa sulks and says, "If you really cared about me, you'd massage my back like I asked you."
**Assertive response**: "I'd love you to massage my back before we make love—it helps me to relax."

**Scenario 3:** Diane wants to make love in the living room, but her partner Lewis seems resistant.
**1.** Diane says accusingly, "I'm really fed up—you never do what I ask."
**2.** Diane hints, "Instead of going to bed early, shall we stay downstairs for a while?"
**3.** When Lewis suggests heading upstairs for bed, Diane replies, "I think I'll stay down here."

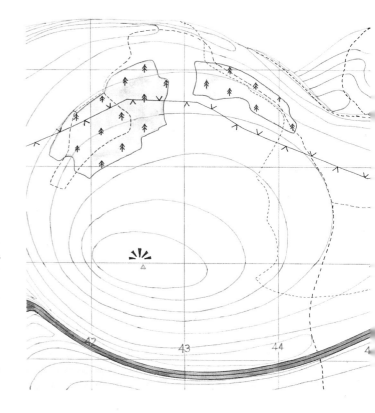

**Assertive response**: When they are relaxing together, Diane approaches Lewis gently: "You seem to feel uncomfortable about making love downstairs. Can we talk about it so I can understand?"

**Scenario 4:** Mike wants Liz to stroke his penis more firmly. He has tried before to tell her what he wants, but her touch is still too light.
**1.** Mike complains, "You'll never do this right. Why don't you just give up?"
**2.** Mike pushes her hand away impatiently, saying "Don't bother—it doesn't matter."
**3.** Mike puts Liz down, saying, "My ex-wife knew exactly what I like. I didn't have to keep telling her."
**Assertive response**: Mike tells Liz, "I love it when you stroke me really hard." At the same time, he shows her exactly what he means by putting his hand over hers as she grips him.

**Scenario 5:** Anna and Mark have been together six months. Anna wants to try using a vibrator, but Mark refuses. She asks why.

**1.** Mark says defensively, "What's so wrong with my lovemaking that you need a vibrator?"
**2.** Mark states flatly, "I'll think about it after we've been together a year."
**3.** Mark refuses to consider the matter, claiming "Vibrators are too impersonal."
**Assertive response**: "I've never used a vibrator, so I feel really nervous about it. Maybe we could try it once, then discuss it again."

**Scenario 6:** Ed often creeps up and grabs Carol's breasts from behind. She wants him to stop:
**1.** Carol declares agressively, "If you do that once more, I won't make love with you for a month."
**2.** Carol squirms out of his grasp without saying anything, but she sulks for the rest of the evening.
**3.** Carol says sarcastically, "Aren't you subtle?"
**Assertive response**: Choosing a quiet time, Carol explains, "When you do that, I feel violated and angry because you are treating me like an object— you don't seem to consider how I might react to such a gesture."

*Finding the way*
*You cannot expect someone else to know what you want by magic—you have to show or tell your partner clearly the way to please you.*

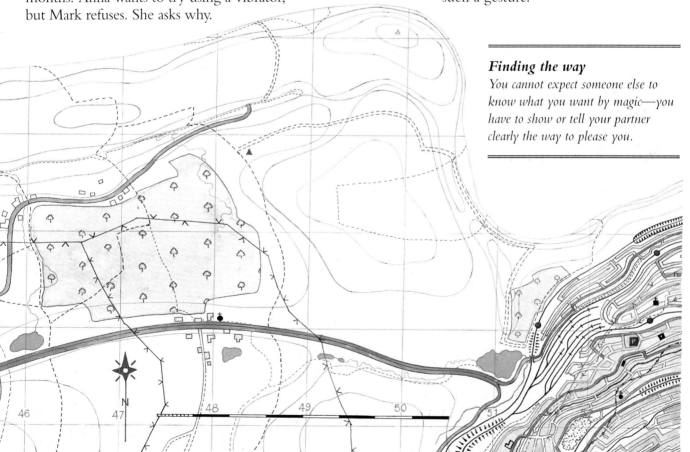

# YOUR SEX QUERIES ANSWERED

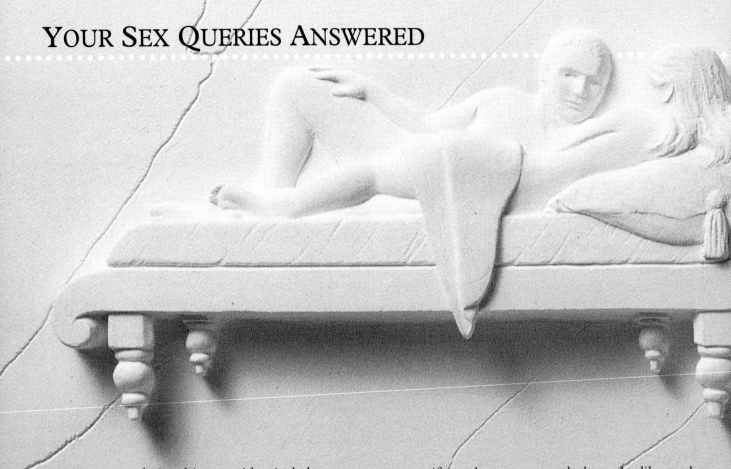

No two relationships are identical, but certain sexual difficulties affect all sorts of couples at some time in their lives. These common problems usually stem from misunderstanding or misapprehension rather than a fundamental lack of sexual compatibility.

## Why can't I satisfy her?

Question: My wife and I both enjoy lovemaking, but no matter which position we try, or how long I am able to thrust into her without coming myself, she never achieves orgasm. She becomes aroused when I stroke her clitoris, but we both feel she won't have experienced a "real" orgasm until she reaches it through intercourse alone.

Answer: The idea that a woman should automatically be able to achieve satisfaction through penetration alone is a common fallacy. Although some women can reach orgasm this way, many need more direct or indirect stimulation of the clitoris right up until the point of orgasm. Experiment with positions that enable you to do this while you are penetrating her: Entering her from behind or letting her sit astride you, for example, will leave her clitoris free, so you can stimulate it, or she can do this herself. Encourage your wife to show you exactly how she likes to be touched and to tell you when you caress her in a way that she finds particularly arousing.

## Partner or plaything?

Question: My partner and I have always been fairly relaxed in our attitude to sex, but I was shocked recently when he asked me to wear stockings and suspenders while we make love. He claims it would be only "a bit of fun," but the idea makes me very uncomfortable—it's as if he sees me as a sort of girlie pin-up rather than a partner. I'm also afraid that he no longer finds me attractive and that I have to dress up in order to excite him. This conflict is creating tension between us.

Answer: This problem reflects one of the basic differences between men and women—the way they are aroused sexually. On the whole, men are more responsive than women to visual stimuli, whereas women are more affected by touch and smell. The fact that your partner wants you to dress provocatively, therefore, is not necessarily an indication that he sees you as a sex toy, or that he is not attracted to you any more. Once you have accepted this, you may find it easier to try going along with his request in order to please him. If you still feel unhappy about the idea, however, it's important that you explain this in a calm, non-confrontational way, without criticizing him for expressing his feelings, or making him feel guilty for asking you to go along with them. If there is some other form of sex play or variation that you'd like to try, suggest this instead, so he will know you have a positive interest in making your sex life good for both of you and are not just reluctant to try anything new.

## Premature ejaculation

Question: I have recently started seeing a woman and we have slept together a few times. I find her very sexy and I suspect that she has a very high sex drive. The problem is that I think I'm coming too soon. I have had this problem before at the beginning of a relationship, but it has always worn off. But I feel so nervous about whether I can satisfy her in bed that I can't see the situation's improving.

Answer: You can tackle this problem on two fronts. First, you need to reduce your own anxiety—if you are anxious, it will be hard for you to relax during sex and you are even more likely to come before you want to. Always take plenty of time over foreplay. If you can arouse your partner well, and perhaps stimulate her so that she climaxes before intercourse, you will feel more confident that you are pleasing her and so be less tense.

You can also improve your physical control over your climax using the stop-start technique. With this procedure, you gradually increase your ability to delay ejaculation, progressing in stages to full intercourse. The first exercise is to masturbate by yourself; as soon as you feel that you are about to ejaculate, stop and relax. Start again when you no longer feel close to orgasm. Repeat this procedure, delaying ejaculation for at least 15 minutes. Do this exercise a few times, then try the same thing using a lubricant jelly to intensify the sensations while practicing maintaining control. Then move on to trying to delay your orgasm by varying the pressure or tempo rather than by stopping. As you increase your control, you will become less nervous about performing. If your partner is sympathetic, she will want to help you and you can continue the stop-start technique during intercourse initially, too.

## Separating fact from fantasy

Question: My partner and I recently admitted to each other that we both sometimes indulge in sexual fantasies to heighten our arousal and help us achieve orgasm. At first, we enjoyed discussing these fantasies, but when she described one in which she was having sex with another woman, I was horrified. Surely, the fact that she thinks about things like this indicates that she is not satisfied by our lovemaking. I'm also beginning to feel as though my masculinity is under threat.

Answer: It's extremely unlikely that your partner's lesbian fantasy threatens either your relationship or your sexual identity. While many people fantasize frequently without ever involving their partner, others find that sharing their fantasies enhances their sexual relationship. In order to do this, it's important for both partners to realize that, in general, fantasies like the one you describe are not exercises in wish fulfillment—one of the main reasons why fantasies are so exciting is that they are not real, and are not intended to become real.

## Fear of failure

Question: My husband and I have been married for four years. A few months ago, he lost his job, and has not been able to find another one. At first we coped quite well, but our relationship has gradually become more strained, and recently, he has begun to lose his erection during sex. The first few times this happened, I was not too concerned, but I'm starting to feel hurt and rejected, and I feel that he no longer finds me attractive.

Answer: It's much more likely that your husband's loss of erection is a direct result of the fact that he is unemployed. Many men equate job success and status with self-esteem, and their sexual self-image can take a severe knock when they find themselves out of work. What your husband needs most from you now is patience and understanding.

Take the pressure off him by agreeing that the next few times you make love, you will not attempt intercourse: arouse and stimulate each other, but put a temporary ban on full intercourse. This will help reduce any "performance" anxiety he has. It is also important to bolster his self-esteem. Encourage him to pursue any interests he has more actively, such as a sport, craft, or some form of further education. If the problem persists, you should consult a sex therapist together.

# GET THE BEST OUT OF IT

HAVE YOU EVER watched a steamy sex scene at the movies or on television, and suddenly felt that your own sex life was boring and monotonous in comparison? Whether you are middle aged or in the first flush of youth, whether you possess the face and body of a film star, or the average assortment of human imperfections, there is no reason why your lovemaking should not be just as exciting, varied, and passionate as anything portrayed on the screen. The most important difference, of course, is that your passion can be for real.

Achieving this, of course, is less a matter of flawless beauty and skillful technique than of real closeness, commitment, and communication. As a bonus, you may discover that the increased intimacy that comes from identifying, sharing, and solving any sexual problems you and your partner may have, enhances every aspect of your relationship considerably.

## Finding the time

One essential element of a fulfilling sex life is time; it's very difficult to enjoy making love unless you feel rested and relaxed. This immutable fact is responsible for a wide range of sexual problems because so many couples establish a pattern of making love last thing at night, when they are both worn out from working long hours and often caring for a young family as well. By the time they turn to each other, they are interested only in sleep. What's more, at the end of the day people are often preoccupied with details of their professional or domestic life—if an important project will be finished on time, perhaps, or whether a fractious baby is likely to wake. It's not surprising that one or both partners find it difficult to tune in to their own—and one another's—sexual feelings.

One way to approach this "tiredness trap" is to set aside special times for lovemaking. If you think

this sounds like too much trouble, or fear it could spoil the spontaneity of sex, reflect on the early days of your relationship. You and your partner probably felt hugely excited before each meeting, largely because you both knew you would end up making love. This advance knowledge, far from making the situation false or contrived, added an extra *frisson* of its own. To recapture this, agree with your partner a time when neither of you will be exhausted, and you can enjoy at least an hour of uninterrupted time together. If this sounds excessive, keep in mind that you may want to spend a little while just talking quietly before you even begin to make love.

## Setting the scene

Another key to satisfying sex is environment. Do you always choose the same room as well as the same time? If so, you can alter the atmosphere considerably by leaving one soft, romantic lamp on, or by lighting a single fat candle or a cluster of smaller ones. To add a touch of subtle fragrance, invest in a scented candle or oil burner. If you always make love in bed, try using a comfortable chair instead, perhaps choosing a seated, woman-on-top, position for intercourse. Alternatively, make love on the floor, softening the hard surface with a duvet, a blanket, or a pile of cushions. Or experiment with several different locations around the house to establish those that are warm and comfortable enough to provide a relaxing environment, yet at the same time offer the stimulation of change.

### Behind the scenes
*Romantic relationships are never as perfect and problem-free as those in fiction and fairytale; they exist between real human beings in the context of everyday life.*

## Mind and body

One of the most important elements in a healthy, mutually satisfying, sex life is both partners' level of self-esteem, particularly in terms of their own body. It may not be possible for you to change your appearance dramatically, but it's worth learning to accept and appreciate the body you have. Otherwise, you risk destroying the spontaneity and freedom that are so vital in a sexual relationship by constantly worrying about sucking in your stomach, or concealing your thighs from view. Remember that if your body were undesirable, your partner wouldn't want to make love with you.

To increase your sensory awareness and ease yourself into a relaxed and responsive mood, begin by soaking in a warm, scented bath. Afterward, reinforce the feeling of sensuality by massaging a little of your favorite oil or lotion into your skin. Even when you can't spare enough time for this degree of pampering, however, you'll feel much more at ease when you are freshly washed with clean hair and teeth. Out of consideration for their partner, men should make sure they are cleanly shaven; similarly, many women wax or shave their legs regularly to avoid bristly stubble. Some people find it rewarding to wear particular items of clothing—anything from a pair of jeans to an array of silky underwear—that their partner finds especially arousing. Although most couples occasionally enjoy sex when they are sweaty and dressed in old clothes, intimacy tends to be much more pleasant when both partners are clean and well groomed. What's more, investing the small amount of extra time this involves sends a clear message of care and respect to your partner.

Occasionally, of course, you could turn these preparations into a kind of foreplay. For example, ask your partner to wash you slowly and gently in the bath, or arrange to take a shower together, using a hand-held spray to direct water over your partner's body, perhaps aiming it directly at the breasts, clitoris, or penis. Remember, however, that an excessively powerful jet could inflict more pain than pleasure.

## Filling your needs

Making time for sex and creating the right environment in which to enjoy it, are both very important, but neither of these elements is of any use if the act itself is brief, boring, or distasteful for either partner. Of these possibilities, per-

### Making time for sex
*The reality of relationships is that sex is just one of the many aspects of a busy life. It is important to make time for sexual enjoyment rather than allowing yourself to become submerged in a mundane routine of work and household chores.*

haps the most common complaint from couples experiencing sexual problems is that their lovemaking is over too quickly. If this is a problem area in your relationship, try agreeing with your partner that a specified amount of time—say half an hour—will be devoted to cuddling, touching, and kissing before you go on to intercourse. With this kind of arrangement in place, both partners can feel secure in the knowledge that there will be plenty of time for exploring each other's bodies and experimenting with different kinds of stimulation. Try to tune in closely to your partner's responses, and encourage him or her to tell you what is especially enjoyable. In turn, let your partner know if there is anything that gives you particular pleasure or makes you feel uncomfortable. Do this sensitively, without being

overly negative or critical. One useful tactic is to place your hand over your partner's, and demonstrate the type of pressure or touch you prefer. This degree of close and clear communication during sex can forge a strong and deep understanding between lovers, especially during periods of growth and change, when their sexual needs may alter considerably. The absence of such communication is responsible for the fact that so many sexual relationships become hidebound and stale. Such sexual stagnation is one very common cause of infidelity; in an illicit affair, any lack of real understanding can easily be concealed by the thrill of passion and novelty. It's common for couples to hold the idealistic and mistaken belief that their initial degree of sexual intensity should last for ever, and that if it

### Domestic scenes
*Satisfying communication and lasting intimacy are possible only in real relationships—those that exist among the problems and confusion of everyday life.*

starts to fade, the relationship is effectively over. In fact, the excitement and novelty of a new relationship can never, by definition, be sustained indefinitely. At the same time, no brief liaison can offer the warmth, intimacy, trust, and security of a healthy emotional and sexual bond that has had time to develop and mature.

## Sex in context
In many sexual relationships, the most neglected element is the context in which it takes place. This is largely because of the different ways that men and women perceive sexual behavior. For most women, sex is inextricably linked to emotion and mood, and this is why they complain when men expect sex even when the atmosphere is tense as a result of an argument, or immediately after a long period of separation. Generally, for women, making love is a culmination of increased feelings of closeness over a period of time, so they are less likely to respond to sexual advances if they have had little affection or attention beforehand.

Men, in contrast, are likely to use sex *instead* of talking or cuddling as a way of demonstrating love and affection. When a woman does not respond immediately, her partner can feel perplexed and hurt, interpreting this perceived lack of interest as personal rejection. The only way to sort through these misread signals and mixed messages is to work hard at communication in every area of your relationship, not just in bed.

Any effort you make is bound to be worthwhile: Although it sometimes seems as though Western culture has debased sexuality by overexposure, pornography, and cynicism, it retains its position at the heart of most loving partnerships. Creating a strong and lasting sexual relationship will help any couple to achieve the kind of intimacy that is only possible when fear and insecurity have been overcome. In the same way, feeling completely safe and truly loved is the key to all joyful, fulfilling sex.

# WHAT'S YOUR SEXUAL STYLE?

Like a musical instrument, your sexuality has its own particular style: romantic like a harp, perhaps, or highly exciting like a set of drums. This questionnaire can help you define your sexual style. If you are currently single, answer the questions with reference to your previous relationships.

It's unlikely that all your answers will fall into one category, but a revealing pattern is likely to emerge. Recognizing this can help you improve your sexual relationships.

**1.** To enjoy sex fully, you should be young, with a slim and healthy body ............................... Yes ❑ ..... No ❑

**2.** If you want a happy love life, you must practice a lot .................. Yes ❑ ..... No ❑

**3.** Most people want affection in relationships .. Yes ❑ ..... No ❑

**4.** You should have lots of sexual partners to help you learn what type of sex suits you best ......................... Yes ❑ ..... No ❑

**5.** I get annoyed if my partner doesn't seem to know what he or she is doing ......................................... Yes ❑ ..... No ❑

**6.** I have few complaints from partners about my sexual technique .......................................................... Yes ❑ ..... No ❑

**7.** If something goes wrong in your sex life, you can probably find a book or video that will help you improve it .............................................................. Yes ❑ ..... No ❑

**8.** I don't always ask for sex when I'd like it ..... Yes ❑ ..... No ❑

**9.** You automatically know when you meet the right person for you .......................................................... Yes ❑ ..... No ❑

**10.** Sex can help any couple to feel closer, and keep their relationship alive .................................................. Yes ❑ ..... No ❑

**11.** If your partner doesn't go along with your sexual moods, it can ruin everything ............................... Yes ❑ ..... No ❑

**12.** If you are single, masturbation is a good way to release sexual tension ........................................... Yes ❑ ..... No ❑

**13.** I often read sex manuals to learn new or different techniques ..................................................... Yes ❑ ..... No ❑

**14.** I watch my partner's expression to gauge his or her response during lovemaking ........................... Yes ❑ ..... No ❑

**15.** Putting on a condom may ruin sex because you have to interrupt arousal ............................................. Yes ❑ ..... No ❑

**16.** If your partner does something that doesn't arouse you, you should say so immediately so he or she won't do it again ............................................................. Yes ❑ ..... No ❑

**17.** I often ask my partner what he or she would like in sex ............................................................... Yes ❑ ..... No ❑

**18.** You should always know your partner's sexual history .............................................................. Yes ❑ ..... No ❑

**19.** I know how to arouse my partner ............. Yes ❑ ..... No ❑

**20.** Sex outdoors is exciting, and can help you feel highly aroused .............................................................. Yes ❑ ..... No ❑

**21.** I enjoy watching sexy videos, and like to talk to my partner about them ........................................... Yes ❑ ..... No ❑

**22.** Sex is essentially a biological behavior, so what you think about it is not very important ......................... Yes ❑ ..... No ❑

**23.** I learned through masturbation exactly how I like to be touched ............................................................. Yes ❑ ..... No ❑

**24.** Sex should be spontaneous, and is at its best when unplanned ........................................................ Yes ❑ ..... No ❑

**25.** I would like to watch my partner make love with someone else ...................................... Yes ☐ .....No ☐

**26.** Experimenting with different positions for sex is important to prevent boredom ...................... Yes ☐ .....No ☐

**27.** I would like to make love in every room in the house .................................................. Yes ☐ ....No ☐

**28.** I would never insist on lovemaking if my partner seemed tired or unwilling .............................. Yes ☐ .....No ☐

**29.** It's important to tell your partner your sexual likes and dislikes before you first make love ................. Yes ☐ .....No ☐

**30.** Lovemaking is very often knowing how to press the "right buttons" ........................................ Yes ☐ ....No ☐

**31.** Sometimes I can sense if my partner needs a different type of stimulation during sex........................ Yes ☐ .....No ☐

**32.** Contraception is a vital consideration in any sexual relationship ............................................ Yes ☐ .....No ☐

**33.** Most sexual problems occur because you are with the wrong person.......................................... Yes ☐ ....No ☐

**34.** I can often persuade my partner to make love, even if he or she doesn't want to ....................... Yes ☐ .....No ☐

**35.** I talk to my partner while making love .....Yes ☐ .....No ☐

**36.** Quick sex is usually more intense and satisfying .................................................... Yes ☐ ....No ☐

**37.** Different stages of life probably alter your response to sex........................................................ Yes ☐ .....No ☐

**38.** I understand how my partner's sexual organs work, and the biological process of arousal........................ Yes ☐ .....No ☐

**39.** Sex toys can spice up sex ........................... Yes ☐ ....No ☐

**40.** Sometimes I put my own sexual needs second to my partner's.......................................................Yes☐ .....No ☐

**41.** I fantasize about sexual experiences I have had or would like to try....................................... Yes ☐ ....No ☐

**42.** Good sex only happens when you are truly in love ...................................................... Yes ☐ .....No ☐

**43.** Sometimes a cuddle is as good as making love .................................................. Yes ☐ .....No ☐

**44.** Sex is overrated. There are more important things in life......Yes ☐.....No ☐

**45.** I can control my orgasm to make sex last longer......Yes ☐.....No ☐

**46.** Sexually speaking, women like to be swept off their feet with the man taking charge.............Yes ☐.....No ☐

**47.** My sexual style varies according to my, or my partner's, mood. Sometimes it's quick and lusty; other times it's slow and sensuous.................Yes ☐....No ☐

**48.** If you choose the right person, they will know what type of sex you like......................................Yes ☐.....No ☐

**49.** You should always bathe or shower before making love............................Yes ☐....No ☐

**50.** I have tried most things in sex, and feel OK about it.....Yes ☐....No ☐

*Refer to page 141 to see which sexual style you have, then turn to the next page to discover which styles are compatible with your own.*

# ARE YOU SEXUALLY COMPATIBLE?

Once you have completed the questionnaire on the previous two pages, and checked your answers on page 141, look at the conclusions below. Eight or more "yes" answers in a set indicates that you have a strong element of that particular attitude in your sexual style. Four to six "yes" replies shows that you have leanings toward that area of sexual expression. If you have a mix of all these attitudes, you are probably fairly open-minded and flexible about sex. If you score very highly in one area, then you may need to rethink your approach in order to enjoy a more varied and fulfilling sex life.

**The romantic lover:** A high score here shows that you dream about sex, and probably don't like to think too hard about important basics, such as contraception. You are also likely to invest all your sexual hopes in an ideal lover, rather than trying to identify your own needs. Your most positive feature is that you tend to see the best side of your partner. This could make your sex life enjoyable, but you might be hurt through blindness to your lover's faults.

**The practical lover:** A high score in this set shows that you see sex as part of your life, but not as a highly rated activity. You are probably well informed about the mechanics of sex, but less responsive to its emotional importance for your relationship, and may tend to be unadventurous. You have a responsible attitude and your partner should feel secure that you would take sensible steps to make sure that sex was safe, so that neither of you was open to the risk of sexually transmitted disease or an unwanted pregnancy.

**The skillful lover:** If you have scored highly here, then you may be a "sexual student" who prides yourself on your sexual prowess. You are likely to believe that technique is all-important,

and once learned, you may apply the same routine to all your partners. Your partner may appreciate your sexual skill, but could feel sex is just a performance with you, rather than a natural and spontaneous affair. You need to relax, and feel free to make mistakes sometimes.

**The adventurous lover:** Scoring highly in this section suggests that sex with you would never be dull! You are willing to try out new ideas, and even explore sexual activities others would feel uncomfortable about. You could carry your partners along in your enthusiasm, but you might also turn them off with your demands. You may be taking risks with your sexual health, and could be addicted to the sensation of sex, rather than commited to building a relationship.

**The responsive lover:** A high score here suggests that you are a thoughtful and considerate lover. You see sex as part of the whole relationship, rather than as a separate concern, outside of normal communication. You are usually anxious to please, and willing to learn from your partner's needs and desires, but you may occasionally put your own sexual needs last. Your partner could see you as lacking in sexual dynamism, and want you to express your own appetite more forcibly.

## Finding a compatible partner

The questionnaire "What's Your Sexual Style?" showed you how your sexual attitudes tend to influence the type of sex you most enjoy. Your preferred sexual style can also affect your choice of partner, and even the quality of the relationship. Choosing a partner with sexual views that complement your own may help you have a fulfilling love life. But what do you do if you are with someone who seems completely incompatible? This might happen if your partner comes from a different, or sometimes opposite, category from you. Of course, you may pass through a number of these categories during the course of a relationship. Learning about your usual style, and your partner's, will help you to become more versatile and to respond to your lover in a more flexible way.

Some musical instruments work particularly well together, and the same is true of certain sexual styles. Perhaps the most common, and hard-to-handle, pairing between categories is the romantic woman with the skillful man. She will expect him to be as committed as she is. At first, she may like his view that the man should be in charge. She will expect him to fulfill all her dreams of a strong, but sensitive, hero. Disappointment may follow because he may grow bored of making all the running, and she gradually discovers that his lack of emotion fails to feed her desire for closeness. As a romantic, she may long for him to buy her flowers, and tell her how much he loves her. He is unlikely to do this naturally, but she might influence him by explaining how important small gestures of affection are to her. Skillful lovers tend to respond to clearly expressed needs, rather than being left to guess what their partner is hoping for. This goes against the romantic belief that true love means understanding your partner's needs without being told, but could aid intimacy in the long run.

## A quest for adventure

Adventurous partners are far more likely to stir up trouble in a relationship than any other type. They can seem exciting and daring at first. Their impetuosity may be endearing, but when paired with a practical partner, may be explosive. With their cautious natures, practical lovers can make good foils for skillful or responsive types, but not for adventurous ones. Adventurous lovers will feel stifled by the practical type's attention to detail (especially contraception). They may even grow wilder in an attempt to drag the practical one along with them, but this will only widen the gap between them.

The practical partner's efforts to make the adventurous one calm down are likely to fall on deaf ears, while a responsive partner may feel overwhelmed by an adventurous type, and could end up feeling as though he or she doesn't really exist except to satisfy the partner's demands.

Adventurous types are likely to be young, or perhaps moving on from a long-term relationship. It tends to be the shortest-lived of all the categories, although couples may notice bursts of this style during their relationship.

## Feeling responsive

Responsive lovers are perhaps the most versatile of all the types, as they can integrate change in themselves and their partner with their sexual behavior.

They are willing to try new things, but also take their cue from a partner's changing desires. Romantics make good partners for them, as they often place equal stress on the importance of a loving relationship. Responsive people are likely to find skillful lovers hard to cope with: Their accent on adapting to others' needs is completely opposite to the rule-oriented approach of the skillful partner. They might be able to deal with this by encouraging the skillful lover to let go occasionally, but arguments will probably develop over who should initiate sex, or what actually happens during sex. A responsive partner may feel that caressing is good enough to enjoy on its own, while the skillful lover will insist on moving on to intercourse.

Although examining your sexuality under these categories can help you to understand your basic sexual preferences, you are likely to have elements of all of them during your sexual life. Use your understanding of these different natures to explore sexual communication with your partner—perhaps talking over how to build on new insights. Discuss the attributes and difficulties of your own style, and compare these with your partner's. You should be able to see the strengths you share, and any weaknesses you could work on together.

# FEELINGS THAT SPOIL SEX

WHEN SEX GOES WELL in a relationship, it can help the partnership to stay strong and loving. Equally, unhappy or unsatisfactory sex can make a couple feel that there is little future in staying together, or be such a painful subject that it is never talked about openly at all. In recent years, there has been a strong emphasis on the importance of learning and improving sexual technique. Many couples have found this helpful, but others have found themselves struggling to understand why they are experiencing sexual problems, in spite of becoming more knowledgeable.

In fact, the root causes of recurrent sexual tensions are usually hidden emotions which block sexual fulfillment rather than a lack of expertise. These secret feelings may often appear, at first sight, to have nothing to do with what a couple do in bed together. Suffering a bereavement, moving house, or even getting married, can all cause unwelcome changes in a sexual relationship.

## The effects of low self-esteem

Another factor that might not seem to be related but that can adversely affect a couple's sex life is if either one suffers from depression or low self-esteem. Tricia and Michael's sex life changed dramatically after Michael became depressed. He was withdrawn, and seldom returned Tricia's displays of affection. Tricia realized that he had seemed low since they were both involved in a serious car accident. Although neither had been badly hurt physically, they had both suffered from shock and the car had been written off. Tricia couldn't immediately see how this could have affected their love life. In fact, she felt lucky to be alive. Privately, Michael felt very differently. He blamed himself for the crash, and his self-esteem had sunk very low. Sex was the last thing on his mind.

Michael's doctor was also concerned, and suggested that he see a counselor to talk things over. As Michael began to discuss the effects of the crash with the counselor, he also began to open up to Tricia. Tricia told him that she hadn't understood the depth of his feelings. Together they decided on a bedtime ritual of talking and stroking and cuddling each other. Gradually, their sex life returned to normal. Michael felt better able to respond to Tricia as the weight of his depression began to lift. Michael's feelings about the accident had been frozen

***Muddy waters***
*Unresolved frustrations may erode a couple's desire for each other and inflict considerable damage on their sex life. What's more, worrying about sexual problems may obscure the real cause of the trouble.*

inside, causing him to cut off from all the positive aspects of his life, and concentrate only on his feelings of self-blame. Talking both to the counselor and with Tricia helped him to unlock his more positive side.

## The aftermath of an affair

Seemingly random events can affect any sexual relationship, but sometimes it's obvious what has spoilt a couple's sex life. Both partners may know what has made them feel distanced, but be completely at a loss as to how to improve matters.

Alice and John had been married for seven years when John had an affair with another woman. Alice found out when she received an anonymous letter telling her that John had been seen several times with this woman at a local pub. When she tackled John, he admitted to the affair. For a while, they both felt this would be the end of their marriage. However, John decided he couldn't leave Alice, or their two small children. He finished with his lover, and the relationship seemed to settle down, but their sex life had become almost non-existent. Alice tried to enjoy sex with John, as she had in the past, but often wanted to push him away. John felt disappointed, and unsure how to approach Alice.

After one particularly frustrating attempt at lovemaking, John told Alice he wished he had stayed with his lover. A terrible row developed, during which Alice was shocked to realize just how angry she was about John's infidelity. Alice's hidden anger had made her unable to show John any kind of sexual feelings. She had suppressed her rage, because she felt she should try to rebuild their marriage for the children's sake. All her anger, lack of trust, and desire to punish John, had been channelled into their sex life. When they both calmed down, John explained how he actually felt relieved that Alice had at last shown her true feelings. He had sensed her tension, but was wary of raising the subject because he feared that she would reproach him. Their sex life improved as Alice slowly learned to trust John again. Both went on to understand each other's sexual moods more effectively.

131

## Pressure to perform

Sexual relationships can be adversely affected by changes in the purpose of the relationship. Some couples find that sex is good when they are trying for a baby, but less so at other times. Others find that fear of pregnancy prevents them from really enjoying their lovemaking.

Steven and Clare had been together for two years, when they decided to try for a baby. Using a kit from the pharmacist, Clare calculated the most fertile times of her cycle each month. At first, Steven and Clare enjoyed anticipating sex on Clare's most fertile days. But because Clare looked forward to becoming pregnant, she built her hopes up each month, and was intensely disappointed when her period arrived. She became more and more anxious, and on one occasion called Steven to come home from work to have sex, because she was at her most fertile time. Steven began to feel like a robot, and under pressure to perform to order. He started to make excuses to avoid lovemaking. Clare became more desperate, and they felt distanced and miserable with each other. Neither felt that they could discuss their feelings in case they disappointed the other.

When Clare had not conceived after eight months, they consulted their local Family Planning Clinic. The doctor explained that it was not uncommon for conception to take up to a year to occur. She suggested some relaxation techniques for Clare to practice, because she was obviously tense. She also advised discontinuing the use of the fertility calculator for a while, to help Steven feel less pressured. The doctor promised additional help if Clare had still not conceived within a further few months. Clare and Steven made a conscious decision to make love in a more natural, less planned way. The quality of their love life improved as they became less anxious. Clare became pregnant two months later, and they used their experiences to help them cope with the changes pregnancy brought to their sexual relationship.

## The pull of family ties

Problems within family relationships often affect sexual partnerships. Unspoken resentments that stem from family arguments can come to the surface during lovemaking, because many people's first learning about sexual relationships comes from observing how their own parents interact. If your parents were cool and distanced from each other, for example, then you may also find sharing your feelings with your partner difficult. If the emotional tie between you and your parents is very close, it may be difficult for you to enjoy an adult sexual relationship fully.

Clive and Louise had been going out for several months when Clive asked Louise to move in with him. Louise still lived with her mother, who had been divorced some years previously. Louise and Clive made love when they could, with Louise staying in Clive's flat occasionally. Sex was good, but Clive wanted more commitment. Louise made frequent excuses to Clive about not living with him. Eventually, Louise agreed to move in, but the couple's sexual relationship suffered almost immediately. Louise lost interest in sex, and visited her mother most days—often staying late into the evening. Clive came to resent Louise's mother, perceiving her as being in competition with him for Louise's love. Clive sometimes lost his erection when they made love, but wasn't sure why this happened. Arguments increased between them, and Louise finished the relationship.

Clive and Louise encountered problems because they were unable to deal with the resentment that

## Gaining a clear view

*It is important to identify the source of a problem; once this has been done, both partners can work toward a solution. It is far more effective to target the fundamental cause than to look for a short-term quick fix that conceals the real problem.*

lay beneath their partnership. Louise resented Clive's asking her for more commitment than she wanted to give, and Clive resented Louise's inability to break free of her mother. His erection problems were linked to his anger toward Louise. Louise withdrew sexually from Clive as a symbol of her ambivalence over the relationship as a whole. They might have coped with their problems by allowing each other more sexual space and discussing their expectations of each other, but the foundations of the relationship needed more fundamental work than they were prepared to do.

## The legacy of guilt

Everyday stresses and strains may drain a couple's sexual desire. If these problems are linked to guilt, sexual feelings will be crushed beneath the weight of trying to hold a partnership together.

Jamie and Pat had both worked full-time for the three years of their marriage. They had a good lifestyle, with holidays abroad and meals out, and the finances available to decorate their house as they chose. Then Pat was made redundant, and everything changed. Jamie's work meant that they could still manage, but they could no longer afford expensive meals and holidays. Jamie felt sorry for Pat, and did all he could to reassure her about the situation, but Pat felt extremely guilty, and saw their change in lifestyle as all her fault.

The more Pat worried, the worse their sex life became. She forced herself to make love, but often felt "cut off" from Jamie's touch. She stopped having orgasms, and Jamie wondered if he was doing something wrong. This went on for weeks, until Pat blurted out her feelings to Jamie. He was able to help her with her guilt and loss of self-image by listening patiently and offering reassurance. Pat felt relieved that he had taken notice of her emotions, and didn't blame her for the drop in their income. They decided to improve their sex life by including more massage and touching that would give Pat plenty of time to feel aroused.

## Forging solutions

If a couple's sex life has been happy and satisfying, then goes through a bad patch, other factors are likely to have caused, or at least contributed to it. In some cases, these may involve a change in circumstances—increased pressure at work, for example—that might simply make you tense and tired, impairing your sex drive and ability to relax. If you have ruled out factors of this kind, however, it's wise to look at other areas of your relationship. Are there any deeper concerns than just the immediate sexual worries? Of course, not all couples find that problems in other areas cause sexual difficulties; many discover that successfully working through trials together enhances their sense of trust and closeness, and even enriches their sex life.

# SOLVE YOUR SEXUAL PROBLEMS

If you had a physical complaint, you probably wouldn't hesitate to consult a doctor, but would you be equally happy to see a sex therapist or counselor if you had a sexual problem? Many people simply find sex too embarrassing to discuss and, with the constant diet of idealized, glamorous sex served up by the media, few of us are willing to admit that our sex lives are anything other than ecstatic. But sexual difficulties affect everybody at some time in their lives and they arise in happy relationships as well as relationships that are experiencing problems.

Sexual problems usually stem from one of three main causes: Psychological causes are probably the most important and the most common; for example, if you

were brought up to believe that sex was dirty and taboo, you might find it very difficult to let go sufficiently to enjoy sex fully. In some cases, there may be a purely physical cause: Alcohol can affect a man's erection, while painful intercourse could be due to an infection or insufficient lubrication. Problems such as a lack of orgasm or low arousal often stem from inadequate communication about what excites and pleases you, or a limited knowledge of sexual techniques.

Whatever the problem, getting it into the open limits the damage it can cause to your relationship. Communication is vital: without it, suppressed feelings of anxiety, frustration, and anger are likely to exacerbate the situation.

***Trapped and frustrated***
*If you suffer from a sexual problem you can feel as though there is no hope of finding a way out.*

Even if a problem physically affects only one of you, it may also be very difficult for the other partner. Worrying about satisfying your partner will adversely affect your ability to relax and your libido, reducing the pleasure for both of you. Whether the difficulty is obviously a joint one, such as a difference in sex drives or conflicting sexual preferences; or an individual one, such as impotence or frigidity, it must be addressed by both partners. Many couples find it helpful to see a sex therapist together. This allows them to air their feelings in a neutral setting and also provides practical help in the form of exercises and techniques to try that increase satisfaction for both partners.

Temporary sexual problems are often caused by a change in circumstances: Your sexual desire and responsiveness may drop if you are particularly tired, stressed, or anxious about something else, for example, or if you are living somewhere which doesn't allow you enough privacy to relax. This type of problem should recede naturally when your circumstances improve again.

The following physical problems are quite common. In some cases, you may be aware of an underlying psychological cause or outside worry that is contributing to the problem. If you fear that there might be a physical cause, however, consult your doctor first before considering other possible causes or seeking sex therapy.

## Male sexual problems

These fall broadly into two categories: erection and ejaculation problems. Loss of erection can occur as a natural response to tiredness, stress, or excessive alcohol. Most men experience problems occasionally, but if it is a persistent worry, it should be dealt with; if ignored, it can become an automatic response partially triggered by the anxiety about performing. To break the vicious circle, both partners need to remove the pressure to perform. Replacing intercourse by stroking and touching

### *The joy of talks*
*Talking through sexual problems helps you counter hidden fears and frustrations.*

sessions may help to relax the man until he becomes more confident.

Premature ejaculation—when a man ejaculates before he wanted or planned to—often affects young men, but can happen throughout a man's sexual life. Help lies in teaching a man to recognize the point of no return for ejaculation and using a technique such as "stop-start" (see p.121) to delay his climax. A much less common problem is retarded ejaculation, where a man cannot ejaculate inside his partner at all, or takes so long to ejaculate that both partners become sore. This may be due to a physical problem and should be discussed with a doctor before any other approach is tried.

## Female sexual problems

A number of women find that, even though they become highly aroused, they are unable to climax, while others gain no pleasure from sex at all. Many women are helped by learning more about what excites and stimulates them, experimenting with masturbation, so that they can show a partner how to arouse them.

Vaginismus is a condition where the muscles around the vagina tighten involuntarily, making intercourse painful or impossible. It may occur in women from very sexually repressive backgrounds or women who have suffered a painful or traumatic sexual experience. It is best treated by a sex therapist, who will be able to suggest a series of exercises that gradually reduces the fear of penetration and aids relaxation.

If intercourse is painful—a condition called dyspareunia—it should be investigated by a doctor, because it is often associated with physical problems, such as stitching that has not fully healed after childbirth. A woman may also suffer pain if she is not sufficiently aroused before intercourse: she will not be lubricated enough, so sex will be painful; this can be helped by improved sexual foreplay and by using a vaginal lubricant.

# WHEN THE CHEMISTRY CHANGES

The early stages of a relationship are often characterized by a heady sexual attraction that can be almost overwhelmingly intense. For most couples, this is impossible to sustain, and if there is a decrease in desire, it is easy to fear that this is because your partner is "wrong" for you in the long-term. But even the best-matched couples experience vicissitudes in their sex lives. The idea that sex will be perfect forever if you are right for each other is nothing more than a myth. If you go off the idea of sex with your partner, it certainly doesn't mean that you should abandon the relationship.

## How sex can change

As with any activity that you do regularly, sex between regular partners can easily become routine, predictable, and lacking in excitement. Arousal may be slower and less automatic. The pattern of your lovemaking may seem as regular and uninspiring as doing the Saturday shopping. On the plus side, however, the increased familiarity between partners can lead to a greater awareness of each other's desires and responses and a more relaxed, intimate closeness.

Many people believe that this maturing of their sexual relationship is a direct consequence of growing older, or changing from being a couple to becoming a family. Although men and women do experience physical changes as they grow older in the way they respond to sex, in fact there is no biological reason why you cannot continue an active sex life well into old age. The real reasons why changes in sexual desire happen are much more likely to be concerned with the pressures of modern living, a lack of flexibility in lovemaking, pressures from career and family responsibilities, and less free time in which to relax and enjoy sex. A loss of desire may follow certain significant life events, such as a bereavement or birth, but sometimes it seems to have no particular cause at all.

## Spice up your sex life

If your sex life has lost its sparkle but you feel sure that this is not a symptom of some deeper problem in the relationship, you may be able to reinvigorate it quite simply. This doesn't mean that you need to swing from the chandelier or dress up in leather—just that you are prepared to use your imagination and are willing to have an open mind about trying new approaches to having sex together.

When you discuss the subject with your partner, emphasize the positive; if you start with fault-finding or phrases like, "Why won't you ever make love except on Saturday night?" you are bound to put your partner on the defensive. Instead, focus on something that excites you or that you would like to try: "You look really sexy in that outfit—I'd love us to make love while you're wearing it." Of course, sexual tastes differ from person to person, so if your partner doesn't want to try something you suggest, never make him or her feel inadequate. Similarly, if your partner wants you to do things you are not comfortable with, try to explain this and suggest other things you could try instead.

## ACTIVE AND PASSIVE ROLES

This exercise will increase your awareness of what pleases you both. Take it in turns for one of you to be the active partner, while the other remains totally passive. When you are active, do anything you can think of to please or arouse the other; the passive partner must not participate, even if he or she becomes very excited, but can comment on what the other does: "That's lovely, but it's too gentle; can you press more firmly." If you feel awkward about expressing your wishes, guide your partner with your hands. After an agreed time, reverse the situation so that the passive partner becomes active and concentrates on giving rather than receiving pleasure.

The following suggestions are ideas that may give a lift to your sex life. Try as many as you feel comfortable with, according to your taste. They may also encourage you to think of other things that you would like to do together.

• Massage your partner, using scented oil. Try rubbing, stroking, and kneading, varying the pressure and pace of your movements. Massage every part of the body, including the feet and hands.

• Take it in turns to caress each other with different fabrics, such as silk, angora, and velvet. Try other objects, too: roll an apple down your partner's back or tickle him or her with a feather boa.

• Have a long, candlelit bath together at a time when you know you won't be interrupted. Take plenty of opportunity to pamper yourselves—shampoo each other's hair, scrub each other's back, dry each other with fluffy towels.

• Experiment with touching your partner's body in new ways—stroking with your hair, rubbing with your feet, or nibbling softly.

• Keep some of your clothes on for a change: partial clothing can be more sexy than total nudity.

• Try a new location. If you always make love in bed, try the bathroom floor, a dining-room chair, the shower, or the stairs.

• To add a sense of urgency, limit the duration of your lovemaking; for example, pick a time when you could be discovered after, say, ten minutes.

• Use games to increase the play element of your sex life. Play hide-and-seek—if you find your partner within five minutes, you win a sexual favor. Or, the first person to spot a licence plate starting with a certain letter can choose where to have sex.

• Have an indoor picnic with whatever food makes you feel sexy: strawberries, crusty bread, quails' eggs, marshmallows, peaches. Don't worry about getting crumbs everywhere—you will, but you'll have fun doing it.

• Drizzle cream, honey, or wine onto your partner's nipples, navel, or neck—anywhere you'd like to lick it from.

• Send each other explicit notes saying what you would like sexually. Slip a saucy note into his pocket or shoe; secrete a love message inside her purse or lingerie drawer.

• Have a secret, innocent-sounding code word or phrase that tells the other person that you are thinking about sex.

The secret of enjoying sex throughout your relationship is to remain adaptable, and to talk about sex regularly. If you assume that what you enjoyed ten years ago will do for the next ten, then your sex life will gradually fizzle out. Remain open to new ideas if you want to have a fulfilling sex life that lasts as long as you are together.

# SOLUTIONS

## Page 44:
## Are you a love junky?

Score 1 point each time you answered Never,
2 points for Sometimes, and 3 points for Usually.

**If you scored 10-15,** you are not a love junky, but you may still have trouble making healthy relationships. Look closely at your Sometimes answers and consider how they might contribute to your string of brief, fiery relationships. Alternatively, you may avoid being a love junky because you do not thrive on all-or-nothing relationships, preferring to use your head as well as your heart. If so, you may be well on the way to developing a successful relationship.

**A score of 16-20** means you tend to be a love junky. You conduct your relationships on a seesaw of highs and lows that cannot deliver success in love. You may feel stuck in this pattern and aware that you need to understand and change some of your attitudes. Use the information in the rest of Chapter Two to help you do this.

**If you scored 21-30,** you are almost certainly a love junky. You are in love with love rather than with any person, and fly from one partner to the next in order to maintain the intense feeling of falling in love. You may even focus your whole life on the feelings your relationships evoke in you. Look closely at the questions again and try to figure out what is stopping you from developing a close and lasting relationship with a partner. Use the information in the rest of Chapter Two to help you change the way you feel about love.

## Page 82:
## What's bugging you?

Questions to which you answered **a** are easy to resolve: you are concerned simply about the issue at hand. It is best to tackle this sort of disagreement by stating exactly what it is about the particular problem that bothers you, and then negotiating your differences rather than arguing about them. Don't let the discussion escalate into mutual criticism; instead, try to restrict your comments to stating why you object to a specific element of the other person's behavior and how it makes you feel. You must be prepared to compromise—for example, if you tend to stay out late, you might agree only to do this on certain days or always to phone by an agreed hour.

Questions to which you answered **b** or **c** reveal more complicated issues, which will never be

resolved until you confront them directly. Look carefully at your answers to see whether there is a pattern to them: Do you tend to feel that your partner undervalues you, for example; or that your partner's demands and expectations are curtailing your wishes or independence? Choose a time when you are both calm to discuss these issues, focusing on how you feel and what changes you would like to make rather than blaming your partner (see also "The Art of Negotiation," pp. 100-103). State your thoughts and feelings as clearly as you can: You cannot assume that another person knows how you feel, no matter how close the two of you are. Equally, you must allow your partner to have his or her say, and listen carefully. Often, major arguments stem from quite basic misunderstandings; good communication can help defuse even the most explosive situation.

## Page 112:
## Test your sexual knowledge

**1 b.** Over the last 40 years, the age at which most people have sex for the first time has gradually dropped from 22 to 17, although some fondling is likely to take place from about the age of 14.

**2 c.** Erections can come and go any number of times without affecting a man's sexual response. In fact, harm is more likely to be caused by the pressure to maintain a firm erection, since this kind of performance anxiety can lead to impotence.

**3 c.** Erect nipples are normally the first sign of sexual arousal in a woman. As she becomes more aroused, the darker area around the nipple (the areola) also swells. The vagina begins to lubricate later, as it lengthens in preparation for intercourse. In both men and women, flushing occurs either slightly before orgasm, or at the climax itself.

**4 b.** The frequency of lovemaking changes as couples progress in their relationships: As a rough guide, the newer the relationship, the more often couples make love. Younger couples tend to have sex more often, but the frequency drops by only one or two times a week as people move from their teens to their mid-forties.

**5 a.** Among heterosexuals, young, single men have more sexual partners than any other group, closely followed by young, single women. The changing roles of men and women has meant that the level of sexual experience is now more equal between the sexes than ever before.

**6 b.** When a woman is sexually excited, her clitoris becomes erect, but once she is fully aroused, it slips under the "clitoral hood," a fold of skin at the top of the labia. This may lead a man to assume his partner isn't fully aroused, and a woman to believe her clitoris is too small to be seen. Although the clitoris is small—about the size of a pea—it is very sensitive, and this hood protects it so it can be stimulated without discomfort.

**7 b.** From a physiological standpoint, penis size has no relevance to the sexual pleasure of either partner. The idea that men with large penises are better lovers is a very old one and may have been linked originally to male self-image, with women being taken in by the myth, partly through ignorance about their own sexuality. This is changing as more is learned about female sexual response.

**8 b.** Many women are able to enjoy sex without always reaching orgasm. Although orgasm may be the pinnacle of sexual pleasure, the warmth that intimacy creates can be just as fulfilling. Men can also enjoy sex without climaxing, but are less likely to allow themselves this experience because of myths about ejaculation (see question 2).

**9 b.** Homosexual men have the same varied repertoire of sexual techniques as heterosexual couples. Anal sex may form part of their lovemaking, but they are less likely to have this type of sexual contact than is commonly believed. Mutual masturbation and oral sex are popular with both gay men and lesbians.

**10 a.** This trick often masks the real reasons why a man is ejaculating too soon. It may work for a few occasions, but it prevents full enjoyment of lovemaking, and could lead to loss of erection as the man finds it more and more difficult to concentrate on sexual pleasure. Men who suffer regularly from premature ejaculation should consider seeking sex therapy, which offers a range of techniques to deal with the problem.

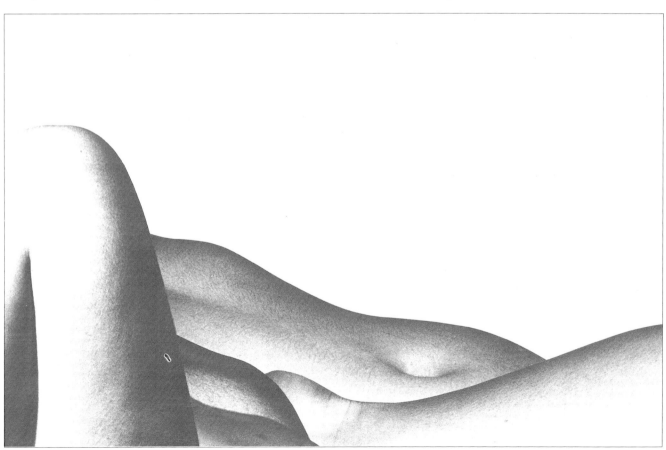

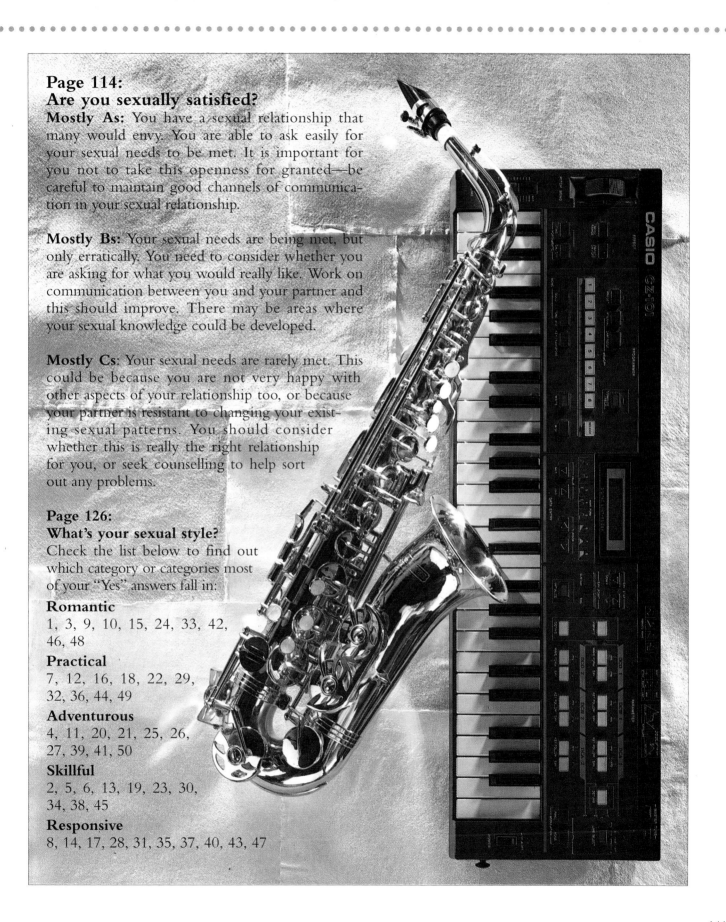

## Page 114:
## Are you sexually satisfied?

**Mostly As:** You have a sexual relationship that many would envy. You are able to ask easily for your sexual needs to be met. It is important for you not to take this openness for granted—be careful to maintain good channels of communication in your sexual relationship.

**Mostly Bs:** Your sexual needs are being met, but only erratically. You need to consider whether you are asking for what you would really like. Work on communication between you and your partner and this should improve. There may be areas where your sexual knowledge could be developed.

**Mostly Cs:** Your sexual needs are rarely met. This could be because you are not very happy with other aspects of your relationship too, or because your partner is resistant to changing your existing sexual patterns. You should consider whether this is really the right relationship for you, or seek counselling to help sort out any problems.

## Page 126:
## What's your sexual style?

Check the list below to find out which category or categories most of your "Yes" answers fall in:

**Romantic**
1, 3, 9, 10, 15, 24, 33, 42, 46, 48

**Practical**
7, 12, 16, 18, 22, 29, 32, 36, 44, 49

**Adventurous**
4, 11, 20, 21, 25, 26, 27, 39, 41, 50

**Skillful**
2, 5, 6, 13, 19, 23, 30, 34, 38, 45

**Responsive**
8, 14, 17, 28, 31, 35, 37, 40, 43, 47

# INDEX

Page numbers printed in *italics* refer to illustrations; page numbers in **bold** refer to self-assessment exercises.

# BIBLIOGRAPHY

Barbara De Angelis, *Are You the One for Me?: Knowing Who's Right and Avoiding Who's Wrong*; Thorsons, London, U.K., 1992

Paul Brown and Carolyn Faulder, *Treat Yourself to Sex—A Guide for Good Loving*; Penguin, London, U.K., 1989

Dr. Eric Berne, *Games People Play: The Psychology of Human Relationships*; Penguin, London, U.K., 1964

Dr. Eric Berne, *Sex in Human Loving*; Penguin, London, U.K., 1970

Jonathan Gathorne-Hardy, *Marriage, Love, Sex and Divorce*; Simon & Schuster Limited, London, U.K., 1981

Celia Haddon, *The Powers of Love*; Michael Joseph Limited, London, U.K., 1985

Susan Jeffers, *Dare to Connect*, Judy Piatkus (Publishers) Limited; London, U.K., 1992

Susan Jeffers, *Feel the Fear and Do It Anyway*, Arrow Books, London, U.K., 1991

Dr. Dan Kiley, *The Peter Pan Syndrome: Men Who Have Never Grown Up*; Corgi Books, London, U.K., 1983

Dr. Dan Kiley, *The Wendy Dilemma: Do You Mother Your Man?*; Arrow Books, London, U.K., 1985

Sarah Litvinoff, *The Relate Guide to Better Relationships;* Vermilion, London, U.K., 1991

Sarah Litvinoff, *The Relate Guide to Sex in Loving Relationships*; Vermilion, London, U.K., 1992

Sarah Litvinoff, *The Relate Guide to Starting Again;* Vermilion, London, U.K., 1993

Pia Mellody, *Facing Love Addiction: Giving Yourself the Power to Change the Way You Love*; Harper, San Francisco, 1992

Anne Moir and David Jessel, *Brainsex*; Michael Joseph Limited, London, U.K., 1989

Robin Norwood, *Women Who Love Too Much: When You Keep Wishing and Hoping He'll Change*; Arrow Books, London, U.K., 1985

George and Nena O'Neill, *Open Marriage—A New Life Style for Couples*; Peter Owen, London, U.K., 1973

M. Scott Peck, *The Road Less Travelled*; Arrow Books, London, U.K., 1990

Judith Pintar, *The Halved Soul: Retelling the Myths of Romantic Love*; Pandora Press, London, U.K., 1992

Victoria Secunda, *Women and Their Fathers*; Cedar, London, U.K., 1993

Sandra Sedgbeer, *Sex, Lies and Love*; Simon & Schuster Limited, London, U.K., 1992

Deborah Tannen, *That's Not What I Meant!*; Virago Press, London, U.K., 1992

Deborah Tannen, *You Just Don't Understand: Women and Men in Conversation;* Virago Press, London, U.K., 1992

Maryon Tysoe, *Love Isn't Quite Enough: The Psychology of Male—Female Relationships*; Fontana, London, U.K., 1992

**CREDITS**

**Illustrators**
Gail Armstrong, David Ashby, David Atkinson, Maria Beddoes, Bill Le Fever, Louise Fairchild, Roy Flooks, Steve Rawlings, John Spencer

**Modelmakers and props suppliers**
Atlas Models, Dualit Ltd, Peter Griffiths, Mark Jamieson, John Lewis Partnership, Revelation Luggage, Mike Shephard

**Photographers**
Michel Focard de Fontefiguieres, Mark Hamilton, Neil Phillips, Mark Preston, Jonny Thompson, Alex Wilson

**Picture sources**
The publishers are grateful to the following individuals and picture libraries for permission to reproduce their photographs:
The Image Bank/*In Focus International*/*Martin Hooper* 98c
Kobal Collection/*Selznick—MGM* 122bl
Frank Lane Picture Agency/*John Watkins* 109br
Frank Lane Picture Agency/*R. Wilmshurst* 109 br
Pictor International 43br
Royal Ballet 28tc
Every effort has been made to trace copyright holders. If there are any unintentional omissions, we would be pleased to insert appropriate acknowledgments in any subsequent editions of this publication.